Dr. Marv Penner

Youth Specialties

ZONDERVAN™

GRAND RAPIDS, MICHIGAN 49530 USA

This book is dedicated to my parents, Irvin and Mary Penner, who showed me good parenting long before there were lots of books and videos on the subject; to my three kids, Tim, Jeff, and Melissa, who have been the brunt of my parenting failures; and to my wife Lois, who is the best parent I know.

Youth Worker's Guide to Parent Ministry: A Practical Plan for Defusing Conflict and Gaining Allies

Copyright © 2003 Youth Specialties

Youth Specialties Books, 300 South Pierce Street, El Cajon, California 92020, are published by Zondervan Publishing House, 5300 Patterson Avenue Southeast, Grand Rapids, Michigan 49530.

Library of Congress Cataloging-in-Publication Data

Penner, Marv, 1951-
   Youth worker's guide to parent ministry : a practical plan for
defusing conflict and gaining allies / by Marv Penner.
         p. cm.
Includes bibliographical references.
   ISBN 0-310-24216-9 (pbk.)
   1.   Church work with youth. 2.   Parenting--Religious
aspects--Christianity.   I. Title.
   BV4447 .P37 2003
   259'.1--dc21

                                            2002012701

Edited by Rick Marschall and Vicki Newby

Cover and interior design by Aaron Vaubel, Design Point Inc., Salem, Oregon

Illustrations by Matt Lorentz

Special thanks for editorial assistance by Lois Penner

Printed in the United States of America

02 03 04 05 06 07 /   / 10 9 8 7 6 5 4 3 2 1

Contents

The Lone Ranger Rides Out of Town

That big white horse in the parking spot marked *Youth Pastor* was mine. The guy in the white hat sitting behind the desk in the office marked *Youth Ministry* was me.

The plot was simple. Young, suave, heroic youth pastor rides into town at sunset to save a whole generation of kids from their pathetic parents and families by providing everything they need to guarantee their personal and spiritual growth through the vulnerable adolescent years.

It seemed so obvious to me at the time. "Everyone knows that parents of teenagers are hopelessly out of touch with their kids' needs," I thought to myself. "They're so focused on managing the trajectories of their careers that they have little time or interest in getting involved in the complicated lives of their own sons and daughters. Absorption in their midlife crises leaves them no energy to invest in the important task of guiding their children into truth. And besides, they don't have the foggiest notion about being cool enough that their kids would like them in spite of their obvious faults."

My task was enormous—be a surrogate parent to a rapidly growing youth group! My role became more overwhelming each day—although the parents seemed enthusiastic about it.

"Go for it, Marv," they cheered as I knocked myself out week after week. The harder I worked to help my students overcome the handicap of their crummy parents, the more bitter I became about what I saw as their parents' incompetence and lack of emotional and spiritual investment.

At least the kids were encouraging. They often told me how much more fun I was than their moms and dads. How much more understanding. How much more in touch with what was happening in their worlds. Their affirmation was the fuel I ran on, and I was working hard to keep my tank as full as possible. What amazed me in the midst of all this was that, in spite of the excellent relational modeling I thought I was pulling off, it seemed the parents were still pulling away from their kids. And they were demanding more from me.

"You need to do better teaching on sexual purity. And while you're at it, tell them they can't date until they're 19."

"Isn't there something in the Bible about kids keeping their rooms clean?"

"I just found a little baggie of white powder in my son's jeans. Aren't you teaching them about drugs down there in your youth group?"

I felt like the guy spinning plates at the circus—frantically running back and forth, trying to keep kids from crashing.

And feeling hopelessly alone in the process.

My epiphany came unexpectedly and quite by accident.

The Turning Point

I had shown a video addressing the issue of teen sexuality at a youth group Bible study. It generated some great discussion among the students, and apparently some of them continued the discussion with their parents at home. Several parents requested an opportunity to see the video I had shown their kids, so I scheduled an evening when they could do just that.

The response was overwhelming. The room was packed with parents, and the lively discussion that followed told me I just might be onto something. As the parents left that evening, they expressed nothing but gratitude and a desire to do it again.

Duh! **What if these parents—whom I had been judging as incompetent, self-centered, and disconnected—were none of these things?**

What if, in reality, they were just afraid, unequipped, and sometimes feeling inadequate for their parenting task? If the latter were the case, my perspective and approach to parent ministry would have to change dramatically. And it did!

Building Bridges with Parents

I began to look for opportunities to strengthen the hand of parents instead of undermining parents' relationships with their kids. It meant a whole different way of thinking about the family, the church, and youth ministry.

The toughest transition was consciously acknowledging the fact that all the kids in my ministry had families. The shape and health of those families varied widely, but that didn't change the importance of supporting rather than replacing them. So I found myself acknowledging, not only the existence of the family, but also its complexity and importance. There was so much to learn.

My first thought was that a lot of the parents needed parenting instruction. I'd been cataloging their failures for several years and was full of advice on how they could improve. After all, my own preschool children made me feel like an expert on all points of parenting, so I couldn't wait to pass on my wisdom.

Needless to say my well-meaning advice didn't receive a warm welcome. **I'd spent so long looking down on parents that they didn't see me as an ally.** Expert advisor was a role I would have to earn.

Investing in Families

It was then that I discovered that the shortest path to the heart of a parent is sincere support and encouragement. If we understand encouragement to mean infusing an individual with courage, the most meaningful ministry that youth workers can have in the lives of parents is encouragement.

I've found that the easiest way to encourage parents is to make positive comments about their sons and daughters. (Now that I've had teenagers of my own, I understand how closely we tie our own sense of self to what's happening in the lives of our kids!) To hear that my daughter asks good questions or provides good leadership or brings a welcoming spirit to a group gives me hope. Most parents are constantly braced to hear bad news about their children—so any good news we can authentically give them is appreciated.

Once relationships with parents are established, there's no group in the world more open and grateful. **Parenting teenagers is a thankless and often lonely job, so our "along side" ministry as youth workers will usually be viewed positively—provided we approach it with a humble and teachable spirit.** But involvement that's condescending and arrogant will send families scrambling back to self-protective postures and may undo whatever trust has been earned.

Through years of trial-and-error experimentation, I've learned that every minute of effort invested in parent ministry pays dividends directly into the lives of kids.

I've also learned that I can do a whole lot more than encourage. In my role of providing an adult voice in the lives of kids, I take every opportunity I'm given to speak positively about parents! An affirming tone in matters related to family is important for this generation as it shapes its attitudes.

Getting parental input on the shape of our youth ministries tells them that their involvement is valued.

Parents are the key faith developers for their children— they can have either a positive or a negative impact on their kid's faith growth. But either way they'll have the biggest impact. You can have strong faith-shaping programs for kids at church, but if you're not partnering with homes you risk producing kids who have a weak faith.

Ben Freudenburg, *The Family Friendly Church* (Group, 1998), page 77

We'll look at practical ways to tap the wisdom and input of parents in later chapters of the book.

As trust grows, we can provide other dimensions of parent ministry. Helping parents connect with each other can create a sense of community and the encouragement that comes with it.

Being viewed by parents as true co-nurturers in the spiritual lives of their sons and daughters may be the highest compliment a youth worker can receive. And involving parents in our ministries means a whole lot more than letting them bring the cookies or drive the van.

The bottom line is basic: we want the students in our care to become all God would have them be. And when that's accomplished by strengthening their families and encouraging their parents to be involved in the process, so much the better.

If our goal is to find fault with parents, we won't have trouble accomplishing it. Most of them are doing the best they can with what they've got and routinely blowing it. Instead I'm asking youth workers to fully adopt a supportive role that frees and equips parents to do a better job in the lives of their kids.

It took me far too long to figure out just how wrong I was about parents. I learned that when you work with parents, you don't always feel like the hero—but seeing a family ride off into the sunset sure makes for a better ending than the Lone Ranger story I was writing.

The white horse and hat are history. Perhaps this book will help you avoid some of the mistakes I've made along the way.

How to Make the Most of This Book

This book is designed to help youth workers develop and implement a plan for a parent ministry that works. Armed with the information presented here, you can reduce the number of problems you face in working with parents by presenting a program that minimizes fear and skepticism and—like the work we do with students—is built on relationships.

As I've already suggested, parent ministry is all about developing trust, gaining understanding, and showing respect. Some of us have barged our way into the lives of parents to point out their mistakes or intimidate them with our supposed expertise, thinking that our primary role is to teach parents how to be better parents. No wonder parents can get defensive at times! Most parents of teenagers won't be particularly excited about getting advice for guiding their kids through the turbulent adolescent years from the parent of a Barney-watching, action figure-collecting four-year-old. Rookie youth workers especially will face challenges in parent ministry that are directly related to lack of experience and, frankly, lack of kids of their own.

Does that mean we shouldn't invest in and minister to parents until we're so old that we can't connect with kids anymore? Of course not! That's the whole point of the book you're holding in your hands. **Every youth worker—young or old, married or single, parent or childless, volunteer or vocational, experienced or just starting out—can be a powerfully positive voice in the lives of parents and families.** It may involve rethinking the way we've typically viewed the parents of our students, but in the long run it will pay huge dividends in our overall ministry effectiveness. Trust me. I've seen it firsthand.

This book presents a deliberate, a thoughtful, and, most importantly, an evolving model for working with parents. It builds a practical strategy that can be implemented by anyone who works with students and their families. The secret lies in following the process as presented in the chapters that follow.

The process assumes that most parents want to have a relationship with their adolescent children and that they're open to help from people like us—when that help is offered humbly and with a desire to strengthen their families. The process also flows from recent research that consistently indicates millennial kids feel positively about their parents in ways previous generations of adolescents haven't. These kids actually like their parents and are more open to letting mom or dad into their lives than we realize. There hasn't been a better time in recent history to free and equip parents for ministry to their own sons and daughters.

I've spoken with too many youth workers over the years who have told me of their failed attempts to enter the world of working with parents.

- "I've tried parent ministry, and it just doesn't work. I put a lot of work into a parent-teen retreat and only three families signed up"

- "I planned an excellent seminar on parenting principles, but the few parents who came just didn't seem to appreciate my insights."

- "I ask them for feedback on the youth ministry program, and all I hear is that it's too expensive."

Unquestionably parent ministry—especially in the early stages—can be a lonely and thankless job. Parents are busy, skeptical, weary of simple answers, and afraid of being associated with a program that could brand them as incompetent or failures. In spite of the early struggles, youth workers everywhere are finding that an investment in parents is ultimately an investment in teenagers. If we're committed to caring for students, we'll do whatever it takes to see them grow.

After we explore some foundational issues, you'll be introduced to a series of levels of parent ministry. The process starts at the bottom of the pyramid where the concepts are basic and the implementation is nonthreatening.

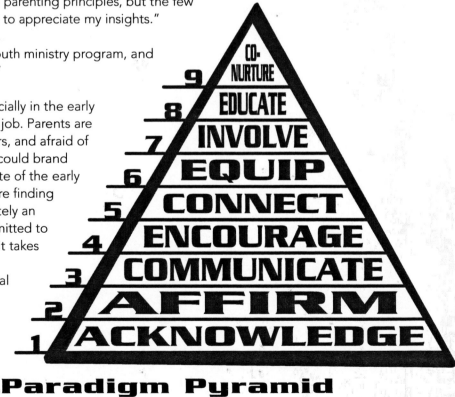

Paradigm Pyramid

9 CO-NURTURE
8 EDUCATE
7 INVOLVE
6 EQUIP
5 CONNECT
4 ENCOURAGE
3 COMMUNICATE
2 AFFIRM
1 ACKNOWLEDGE

Level 9
Co-nurture teens
The youth worker is seen as a partner with a growing number of parents.

Level 8
Educate parents
The youth worker teaches parents of teens in legitimate areas of expertise.

Level 7
Involve parents in ministry
The youth worker finds appropriate ways for parents to participate.

Level 6
Equip parents with tools and information
*The youth worker provides parents with resources to strengthen and equip
them in their parenting role.*

Level 5
Connect parents with each other
*The youth worker finds ways to facilitate relationships between parents for
their mutual benefit and encouragement.*

Level 4
Encourage parents in their role
*The youth worker looks for ways to encourage and bless individual parents
in their relationships with their adolescent children.*

Level 3
Communicate with parents
*The youth worker communicates carefully with parents about every detail of
youth ministry activities and listens carefully to their input and feedback.*

Level 2
Affirm the value of family and parental relationships
*The youth worker takes every opportunity to present parents and the family
in a positive way through attitude, teaching, application, and modeling.*

Level 1
Acknowledge the existence and importance of parents
*The youth worker recognizes that each adolescent has a family context that
matters. The range of family systems must be factored into planning and
programming.*

Each chapter of this book focuses on one level, offering background on that part of the process and practical ideas for implementing it.

Start at the Beginning

The process begins by acknowledging and affirming parents and family. We commit ourselves to listening carefully and communicating clearly. Having established a basis of trust early in the process, we look for ways to encourage parents and connect them with each other. Then we start equipping parents by putting parenting tools into their hands. We look for ways to actively and purposefully involve parents. (You'll be surprised at the variety of ways parents can be involved in ministry.) It's at this stage that we can begin to—humbly—educate parents in areas where we have legitimate expertise.

This approach does not give rise to any parental sense of intrusion, since throughout the process, we acknowledge the importance of parents and our desire to support them. If the process is followed in sequence, parents are more likely to see us as partners with them in ministry, co-nurturers of a new generation who are growing in every area of their lives.

Let me say it again: each level builds on the trust, respect, and rapport created with parents in the previous level. If the levels are allowed to emerge sequentially, a strong, flexible, and effective parent ministry results. Let the model emerge naturally, starting with the bottom levels rather than jumping in with the more intrusive levels near the top. Be patient.

Having said that, realize that none of the steps will ever be fully accomplished since ministry constantly is evolving. You'll have to delve into the communication level before you're finished affirming parents, because you'll never be finished affirming parents. You'll involve parents before you have finished encouraging them, a never-ending process.

Now, let's get started!

• • •

Foundations for Meaningful Ministry to Parents of Adolescents

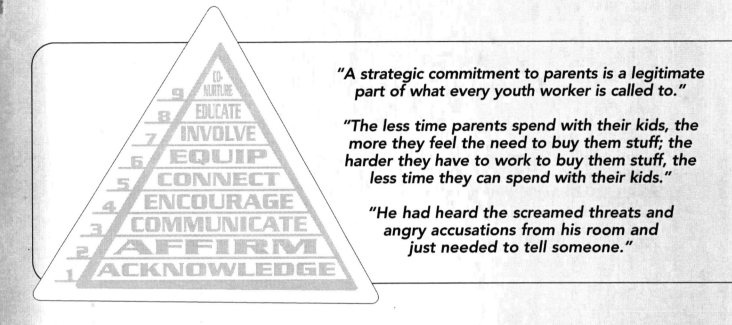

"A strategic commitment to parents is a legitimate part of what every youth worker is called to."

"The less time parents spend with their kids, the more they feel the need to buy them stuff; the harder they have to work to buy them stuff, the less time they can spend with their kids."

"He had heard the screamed threats and angry accusations from his room and just needed to tell someone."

FOUR COMPONENTS OF A HEALTHY CONGREGATION

- A child-, youth-, and family-friendly church
- A parent-empowerment system
- A strong educational ministry for children
- A dynamic youth ministry

Ben Freudenburg, *The Family Friendly Church* (Group, 1998), page 21

Before considering strategies or ministry components, let's take a few minutes to become familiar with the unique world of parent ministry. We'll explore family ministry basics, look at midlife adulthood, and identify eight reasons why parent ministry can be tougher than it looks.

Ministry to Moms and Dads: A Critical Piece of the Youth Ministry Puzzle

Family ministry has become a popular concept among youth workers recently. After decades of departmentalizing and compartmentalizing members of the family, the church is realizing that maybe it's time to start putting the family back together again. Not a moment too soon! Many parents actually enjoy being involved in the lives of their children, and millennial kids welcome parental involvement as no recent generation of young people has. The time is right for an enhanced perspective on family ministry.

In the wake of the tragic school shootings in Jonesboro, Arkansas, in 1998, Pam Carlisle, a Christian teacher whose class walked directly into the line of fire made a powerful statement to the youth workers of North America: "Please see yourselves as a new breed of Christian social workers who are profoundly involved in the lives of the parents of your youth group. Youth ministers must understand that good youth ministry goes beyond the youth group and touches the lives of parents."

Pam was making an observation that many of us who work with students have made. She was suggesting that behind a lot of hurting kids are struggling parents in dysfunctional family systems with relatively few support systems in place to help them. Her thoughts affirm the findings of numerous studies identifying the critical part parents play positively and negatively in the shaping of their children's values and morals.[1]

It's often easy to see the connection in the extreme cases that show up on the front pages of the nation's newspapers, but the facts are that every family has its struggles and no parents or children are perfect. All of us can use help, and youth workers are uniquely positioned to provide it. The secret lies in finding ways to free and equip parents for ministry to their own kids. Freeing parents is the attitudinal component and equipping them is the programmatic component. Both will be addressed in the remaining chapters of this book.

If we're committed to the health and well being of the adolescents in our care, we will seriously consider the place that a conscious investment in their parents will have in our overall ministry strategy. The churches and organizations who hire us may not recognize the value of parent ministry. In fact, parents may not even welcome our involvement (for a variety of reasons to be addressed later). In spite of the obstacles, however,

---

1. See "Teens' Closeness to Parents and School Helps Influence Conduct, Study Shows," *Wall Street Journal*, 10 September 1997, which spotlighted M. D. Resnick, P. S. Bearman, R.W. Blum, et al., "Protecting Adolescents from Harm: Findings from the National Longitudinal Study on Adolescent Health" (*Journal of the American Medical Association* 278:10 (September 1997), 823-832.

   That parental influence is the strongest factor keeping adolescents from delinquent behavior is clear from Sung Joon Jang's study, "Age-Varying Effects of Family, School, and Peers on Delinquency: A Multilevel Modeling Test of Interactional Theory," *Criminology* 37:3 (August 1999), 643-686. More about this study can be found on the Ohio State University research Web site at osu.edu/units/research/archive/adoldel.htm.

   For evidence that parents are critical in the drinking attitudes of their kids, see E. L. Schor, "Adolescent Alcohol Use: Social Determinants and the Case for Early Family-Centered Prevention," *Bulletin of New York Academic Medicine* 73:2 (Winter 1996), 335-356.

THE SURVEY SAYS

The importance of parents in the lives of their sons and daughters was once again affirmed in a recent nationwide study involving thousands of teenagers. George Barna's book, *Real Teens* (Regal Books, 2001) reports the findings of the project. In spite of the fact that adolescents may seem aloof and disinterested in family matters, the research indicates teens view parents in remarkably positive terms.

- Nine out of 10 teens say they are very close or fairly close to their moms, and 75 percent say the same about their dads.
- More than three out of four say their parents have a lot of influence on their thoughts and actions. The next closest influence was friends, which came in at 51 percent.
- When asked what they would like to see changed about their relationship with their parents, the top two answers were more time together and improved communication.

Obviously family relationships are a high priority for this generation of teenagers.

> Both parent and adolescent are simultaneously in unique cycles of growth and change — children in adolescence and parents in what some psychologists call "middlescence."

Merton Strommen, *Five Cries of Parents* (Harper and Row San Francisco, 1985), page 3

a strategic commitment to parents is a legitimate part of what every youth worker is called to and can pay huge dividends in overall ministry effectiveness.

Meet Mike and Molly Midlife: Typical Parents of Teens

Most of us wouldn't claim to be serious about working with students if we weren't willing to take the time to understand all we can about how teens tick. We eagerly read everything we can about adolescent development. We clip articles from newspapers and magazines if we think they'll help us decode this mysterious culture into which we've been called. We explore their hearts, dissect their relationships, evaluate their media, and investigate their values. We recognize the importance of knowing our audience.

The same should be true when we want to have an effective ministry to parents. **It's important to understand what's going on in the lives of midlife moms and dads as we look for ways to support and encourage them in their responsibilities.**

The vast majority of the parents we work with fall into a relatively narrow age range: mid 30s to mid 50s. Do the math. Many started having kids after they hit their 20s; the kids are teens now. That points to the mid 30s. Most of them stop having babies by the time they hit 40, so the mid 50s marks the other end of the range. This period is known as *middle adulthood*.

Like adolescence, middle adulthood is a relatively recent designation, but in the western postindustrial world, it's understood to be a unique developmental phase. If we understand the changes and challenges of middle adulthood, we can be more effective in our ministry to parents. Many midlife adults report that the years of raising adolescents are full of confusion, emotional chaos, and a revisiting of many of the self-image issues of the teenage years. Add to that many of the relational and vocational issues, and we've got some work to do just to understand them.

So what's going on for Mike and Molly Midlife?

First, you can be pretty sure they're living with substantial stress. Their kids are more expensive than ever to feed, clothe, and entertain. Buying them things is the easiest way to reduce the guilt they feel for not spending enough time with them. It's a vicious cycle. The less time parents spend with their kids, the more they feel the need to buy them stuff; the harder they have to work to buy them stuff, the less time they can spend with their kids.

Parents are often over-committed at work, at church, and in their community. Retirement feels like it's just around the corner, but they sense that they're not financially prepared. If their parents are still alive they're probably beginning to care for them. Sandwiched between two dependent generations, their kids and their parents, they have little time to develop their own interests and relationships.

The workplace generates its own uncertainties. Not much is predictable anymore. Lots of experience isn't necessarily an asset in a context where rapid change is the order of the day. Parents may have already been through a few rounds of downsizing and restructuring. They may have found themselves holding the dreaded pink slip or at least feeling increasingly vulnerable to it. If they're middle or upper class, their investment portfolio made them feel like they won the lottery during the tech boom of the late 90s, but as a generation, they lost billions when the whole stock market imploded at it's peak. If they're working class, they hope the government and company programs designed to see them through their retirement won't disappear the same way.

From their midcourse vantage point they have a clear view of the past and a growing anxiety about the future. Parents may be second-guessing both. Their childrearing choices are now beginning to bear fruit. They often wish they could start over and do things differently, but the die is cast. Now all they can do is watch to see what will happen. Marriages, if they've survived to this point—and about half of them haven't—must be reengineered to take the independence of adolescent children into account. Husbands and wives have a need to get reacquainted as friends and lovers. They no longer are just a mom and dad juggling parenting responsibilities. They get tired just thinking about it.

Mike and Molly are living in slowly deteriorating bodies. In spite of optimistic assertions that "life begins at 40," they are painfully aware of as many endings as beginnings. Molly's on a hormonal roller coaster while her body is shutting down its baby-making department, and Mike's feeling the effect of all those sports injuries. Both of them glance in the mirror after a shower and realize that the law of gravity is a force to be reckoned with. It's all downhill from here.

As their kids pull away to establish their own individuated sense of self, Mike and Molly are wondering what their new roles will be. Mike often feels like he needs to find ways to get to know his kids who seem to have become strangers and Molly wonders what her job is now that they don't need her to wipe their noses and tuck them into bed anymore. Chances are they'll

Parents are often tired.

Parents are scared of the future.

Parents love their kids.

Parents are nervous about the world.

Parents are stressed.

Parents wish they had more fun.

Parents are often lonely.

Parents don't always "have it all together."

Parents want to be taken seriously.

Parents, on the inside, often still think of themselves as being in high school.

Chap Clark, *The Youth Worker's Handbook to Family Ministry* (Youth Specialties, 1997) page 125

FIVE CRIES OF PARENTS

- To understand themselves and their adolescents.
- To experience a close and supportive family life.
- To see moral behavior and purpose developing in their children.
- To know how a shared faith can be experienced by their family.
- To know where to turn for help in crisis situations.

Merton Strommen, *Five Cries of Parents* (Harper and Row San Francisco, 1985)

THE GENERATIONAL PERSONALITY OF BOOMERS

- Boomers love growth, expansion, and anything that's big.
- Boomers see themselves as stars of the show.
- Boomers view personal prosperity as their birthright.
- Boomers are introspective self-searchers.
- Boomers refuse to get old.

Adapted from *Generations at Work* by Zemke, Raines, and Filipczak (Amacom, 1999)

---

end up giving their kids too much freedom or too many rules. It feels to them like the right balance is impossible to achieve.

As card-carrying members of the Baby Boomer cohort, most midlife parents today have some generational tendencies that are worth noting as well. They are used to being the stars of the show. In the postwar world into which they were born, they symbolized the prosperity of the new times. In spite of their parents' efforts to make life safe and comfortable for them, they despised "the establishment." They bucked the system in the 60s to create a world of their own…their own music, their own fashions, their own values, and their own language. When it was time to have kids, the birth control pill gave them the power to control the number and the timing of blessed events. If it didn't work out, an abortion could take care of "the problem."

Personal gratification is a core value of the Boomer generation. Unfortunately, raising teenagers isn't always particularly gratifying. That, in and of itself, creates tension, but Baby Boomers hate the thought of being old so staying closely identified with their children is important to them.

And now, just when we're getting used to Boomers, a whole new generation of parents appears on the horizon. The Baby Buster, or Gen-Xers, waited a lot longer to get married (According to the U.S. Census Bureau, the median age for marriage in 2000 was 26.8 for men and 25.1 for women and rising (compared to about 23 for men and 21 for women in the 1970s when most Boomers were tying the knot) so their kids are just becoming teenagers. We'll have increasing number of Gen-X parents, so get ready.

It's tough to project what any generation will be like when they hit midlife (who could have predicted that the give-peace-a-chance hippies of the 1960s would have turned into the materialistic, self-centered Boomers we know today?), but early indicators are that this generation of adults, who report feeling abandoned and disenfranchised by their parents, will try to make sure their kids don't have the same experience. They appear to be deeply involved in the lives of their children, coaching sports teams, volunteering at the school, home-schooling in growing numbers, and finding creative ways to stay involved with their kids. They've always been an intentionally relational generation.

The media has been a huge part of Gen-Xers' lives, so their idea of what family is like has been deeply influenced by Hollywood portrayals and prime-time TV role models. If there's one thing Gen-X parents will be looking for, it's mentors and coaches. The job of keeping them connected with each other and facilitating mutual ministry will be an important part of every parent ministry. My own guess is they will be tougher to connect with than previous generations of parents simply because they don't trust institutions (like the church) and they're self-reliant.

Let's face it: parents of teenagers, no matter which generation we're talking about, are not an easy bunch to connect with. They face many issues developmentally and generationally. Other challenges are associated with parent ministry as well.

Why Parent Ministry Is Such Hard Work

In many ways parent ministry seems like a very logical and common sense approach to nurturing young people in their faith and preparing them for life. Why is it then that many attempts at establishing a ministry to parents are a struggle? Some of the problems are with us as youth workers and others are with parents. The good news is that, when we understand some of the issues, we can usually take steps to resolve the tensions. Here are eight reasons parent ministry may be an uphill battle.

Youth workers have to consider the needs of the whole youth group. Parents focus on their own kids.

When my daughter Melissa was in second grade, her class did a musical production during the school Christmas pageant. The front row of the balcony looked like a press conference at the White House. A crowded bank of camcorders had an equally crowded bank of parents behind it, each leaning forward and squinting through the eyepieces. We had all opted to experience the yuletide extravaganza on a one-inch screen for the sake of posterity. When the evening was over the teacher asked if one of us would get her a copy of the tape so the whole class could watch it the next day. Each of us sheepishly shook our heads; not one of us could oblige her. Each of us had zoomed in on our own kids. We didn't care who was singing the solo. Each lens was focused tightly on the child of the parent hunched over the viewfinder. That's what parents do!

It's no different for parents whose kids populate our youth groups. They see our ministry through the experiences of their own sons and daughters. When their kids are having a good time everything is good. When their kids are having a bad time the youth pastor is an inexperienced loser who should switch to a career in retail.

There are times in youth ministry when decisions have to be made for the best interest of the entire group. Inevitably the

THE GENERATIONAL PERSONALITY OF GEN-XERS

- Xers are skeptical of things that are big, glitzy, and highly structured.
- Xers are deeply committed to community and relational honesty.
- Xers are attracted to the edge. They're comfortable with change.
- Xers aren't interested in being spectators. They want to participate.
- Xers despise labels.

Adapted from *Generations at Work* by Zemke, Raines, and Filipczak (Amacom, 1999)

DEALING WITH ADOLESCENCE

Ways North American adults deal with adolescence:

- Rushing kids to adulthood — pressing to achieve rites of passage as quickly as possible.
- Making the rites of passage unattainable and dragging out the journey to adulthood endlessly.
- Over-identification — being as much like adolescents as they can.
- Trivializing the serious concerns teens have.
- Imposing greater and greater controls, rules, and consequences.
- Detaching relationally and leaving kids entirely on their own.

Adapted from *All Grown Up and No Place to Go* (revised edition) by David Elkind (Perseus, 1997)

decision will be negative for someone. When it's negative for a kid, it inevitably becomes negative for parents.

- The missions trip is scheduled for a week when most of the group can participate, but for the parent whose son is auditioning for the community orchestra that week, it feels like you've made a bad decision.

- You've chosen to do a series of talks on healthy dating relationships, but a few families don't want their kids to date until they're 18. They feel as though you're undermining their standards.

- A girl on the ski trip gets assigned to a chalet with a group she doesn't like, and the whole trip is a failure as far as she and her parents are concerned.

- The guy whose dad bought him a guitar when he was six (so he could use his talents for Jesus someday) doesn't get chosen for the worship team. Dad writes off everything you do in your ministry from that day forward.

Parents will evaluate the ministry on the basis of how their teens experience it or how it meets their teens' current and most urgent needs.

Youth workers might have the inside scoop on family secrets.

As I sat on the platform looking out at the congregation one Sunday morning, my eyes kept going back to Mike's parents. They sat together sharing a Bible during the sermon, whispering back and forth occasionally and looking like everything was just fine. I would have assumed the same except for the conversation I'd had with Mike earlier that week. He told me about the years of constant bickering that had finally erupted into a full-scale war on Tuesday night. He had heard the screamed threats and angry accusations from his room and just needed to tell someone. I had the burden of his family's problems added to an already heavy load of family secrets that came with my job.

There were others I had gazed upon during other Sunday mornings:

- Brenda's dad had a serious drinking problem no one in the church knew about. He was about to lose his job—and maybe his marriage.

- Trevor's mom was going for more tests the following week. It could be cancer, but the family had decided not to say anything until the results came back.

- Vanessa's dad, a respected church leader, was cheating big time on his income tax according to his daughter.

- Leon was standing awkwardly with his parents. He found a stash of pornography in his dad's bottom drawer, and he had asked me a few days earlier whether he should confront his dad or tell his mom and let her handle it.

- Celine's dad was going to court the next week to face charges of sexual abuse with three of his daughters. It was going to be ugly for all of them.

Sometimes the information is overwhelming. **In many cases we know things about families nobody else knows.** It creates dilemmas of confidentiality for us that have no easy answers. How much do we tell the senior pastor? What is appropriate to share with our spouses? What if the advice we gave was wrong?

There are days we might feel more like smacking parents than encouraging them. That can make it tough to think about ways to get involved in their lives.

Youth workers are too busy already and don't have time or energy for more programs.

Most youth workers I know are operating at full capacity. Even volunteers (or perhaps *especially* volunteers) can hardly imagine adding another layer of responsibility and relationships over an already packed calendar. "I can't keep up with what I'm already trying to pull off here," you might hear them say. "Don't tell me about another huge group of people who need my help."

Everyone seems to have an opinion on how we ought to be spending our time and energy. It's easy to fall into the trap of responding to the loudest, most persuasive voice or taking the easiest path. A youth worker who's in survival mode, running from one event to another, juggling appointments and meetings on a day-to-day basis, will rarely find a way off the treadmill. What I'm proposing is that we stop and evaluate where our ministry investment will pay its best dividends and that we carefully consider the benefits of a purposeful parent ministry. It may not be as tough to implement as you might have thought.

If you're an overworked skeptic think about these two ideas: first, **we must recognize that parent ministry is essentially a change in attitude, not necessarily about additional programming.** Some additional responsibilities may be required as family-based ministry progresses, but a great deal can be done in parent ministry without adding a single event or meeting to your calendar. Secondly, an effective parent ministry may reduce the need for some of our current youth ministry programming. If we believe (as most of us say we do) that youth ministry is about relationships, then strengthening a key relationship in the life of a young person might eliminate the need for some of the other programming we do. It can be a case of "working smarter, not harder."

Youth workers often love being needed. When we're insecure, we often shut parents out.

Let's face it. Most of us are far more driven by our need for applause than we want to admit. Our Messiah complex, however subtle, convinces us that we are God's gift to a whole generation, and kids are often quick to affirm that notion.

"I wish my dad could understand me the way you do, Daryl."

"My mom is just so old fashioned. She hates my music. She doesn't understand my friends. If only she could be more accepting—like you are, Holly."

"I don't know where I'd be in my walk with God if it weren't for you, Buck. I just can't talk to my parents about how I'm feeling. I'm so glad you're around."

"Thanks so much for the talk last night, Bobbi. I tried talking to my parents, but they just didn't hear what I was saying. After talking to you though, I know exactly what to do."

Those kinds of affirmation are the fuel many of us run on. When kids let us know how much better we are at relationships than their parents, we may enjoy it a little too much.

So here's the dilemma: if our ministry is to turn teenagers back to their parents and to help parents connect with their kids at a more meaningful level, we're basically reducing their need for us. When we cast their parents in a positive light we may find ourselves receiving fewer positive emotional strokes. Lots of youth workers I know just aren't prepared to put themselves in that position. Being applauded by kids is too important.

Here's where we may need to be brutally honest about our own baggage. We have to ask ourselves whether we have unresolved issues in our own lives that are making it difficult for us to minister without strings attached. Are we driven by an emptiness that's filled when kids need us—or does our love actually overflow from a fullness that comes from a deep and rich relationship with our Creator? We may need to learn to say with integrity like the psalmist did, "Search me, O God, and know my heart; test me and know my anxious thoughts. See if there is any offensive way in me, and lead me in the way everlasting." [Ps. 139:23-34]

Our need to be needed may be the greatest obstacle to establishing a meaningful ministry to parents.

Parents may feel threatened when their kids are drawn to the youth workers.

We've already discussed the fact that many parents of teens find this new stage of parenthood unsettling. They live with more than their share of self-doubt, regret, and confusion. As their growing kids pull away, they often express feelings of fear and failure. They nostalgically talk about the way it used to be when they still knew everything going on in the lives of their kids. Parents of teens may feel that other adults are now more important and are replacing them. They hear their kids speak in glowing terms about a coach, a teacher, a friend's parent, or a youth worker and they feel their role diminishing. The emotions can be intense. Fear and uncertainty can be expressed as anger or contempt.

A good youth worker will try to understand the feelings being experienced by parents during these tough relational transitions and do everything possible to affirm parents and reassure them of their importance in the lives of their kids. Too often youth workers flaunt the special relationship they have with their students, which only exacerbates the problem. Parents who feel threatened by a youth worker will not view that person as an ally and can be unreceptive to ministry efforts directed their way.

As the parent of three kids who have all been adolescents, I can honestly express gratitude for every adult who has made a positive investment in the lives of my children, but I can also understand the frustrating feeling of being out of the loop. When my daughter looks at me with her you-are-such-a-loser eyes and says, "I've gotta talk to Catherine about this," I take a deep breath and remind myself that Catherine can help, I'm still her dad, and she'll be back when she needs someone to pay for her wedding. It's tough for parents to feel like they play second fiddle in the lives of their children. We need to understand how that feeling can impact our ministry with families.

Parents may not respect young youth workers without teenagers of their own.

We're a nation of armchair quarterbacks, experts on how everyone else ought to handle their lives and relationships. As youth workers who observe families, the fastest way to alienate parents is to set ourselves up as authorities on parenting adolescents. The last thing they need is one more voice telling them where they're blowing it and offering theoretical solutions.

The biggest mistake most rookie youth workers make is to assume that parent ministry equals

teaching parents how they could do a better job raising their kids. "Here's how I'd handle that 15-year-old if I were you," we say, cuddling our 15-*month*-old. This is known as a credibility gap!

We often *can* see the mistakes parents are making with their kids. The longer we work with families the more often we'll see destructive patterns of parenting repeated. Our observations may be accurate, and our suggestions might be right on target, *but* until we've walked a block in their Birkenstocks we'd do better to bite our tongues. We can give parents tools for their tasks, but it's always better for a young or childless youth worker to provide resources at arms length. Bring in an expert, provide a parenting workshop, make tapes and books available, or facilitate parent-to-parent ministry. Just don't be the expert on raising teens yourself! Remain teachable, pray for struggling parents, and be patient. If you're still in youth ministry when your own kids are grown up, then you'll have something to say to the parents you're working with, but I guarantee you'll say it with a different spirit than you might as a 20-something!

Notice the hidden bonus: after watching parents with their teenagers as closely as many of us do, we should be well equipped to avoid the patterns we've seen over and over as we parent our own children. Talk with your spouse about what you're seeing and make the adjustments in your own parenting while your kids are young. Be the learner rather than the teacher. And when you see parents parenting well, invite them to become your mentors. My wife, Lois, and I benefited in practical ways by sitting down with the parents we had come to respect over the years and having them teach us what they had learned in raising their own kids. Take advantage of the unique blessing of working closely with parents and families.

Parents may think they're hiring a baby-sitter.
Some parents simply don't understand the role of youth workers, especially a career youth ministry specialist. Perhaps when they voted for the new pastoral staff member, some parents were thinking of hassle-free week-ends and Wednesday nights. They thought they were getting an energetic, young program director who would occupy their teenager for at least a few hours each week and organize a canoe trip and a service project or two each summer. Getting involved in the life of their family is not what these parents have in mind!

Beware of going into a ministry setting where the calendar is king and your ministry is evaluated by the number of activities you can pull off each month. When exploring a potential opportunity for employment, listen carefully to the congregation and ask God for discernment. Are the congregants looking for a shepherd who will care about souls, or are they looking for someone to baby-sit kids on weekends? Communicate your commitment to the families in your care at the earliest stages of negotiating a new ministry position.

Most churches these days recognize the importance of family ministry but individual parents may not understand your job description unless someone makes it clear to them. We know that youth ministry in the new millennium is not a programming job. It's all about relationships. When we nurture relationships with students we can hardly help becoming involved in the lives of those close to them.

Because some of our involvement with families could reveal parental weakness and failure, we may find parents who are defensive and unresponsive. It's not hard to understand why! They may feel that our interest is interfering or intrusive and that we are there to point out their faults rather than to support and encourage them. Most of these folks are not as closed to our care as they may seem. It takes time, consistency, and patience to let them know we're on their side.

The model of ministry presented in this book is meant to build trust and communicate respect. If we take the time to develop a relationship, most parents will gladly accept any help they can get.

Parents may experience a stigma associated with needing help.
In spite of the fact that parents often wish they could get help, most just aren't willing to ask for it. In their minds, needing help means admitting failure. The reason parents may be reluctant to show up at the workshop

on communication is fear that others will think their own family can't communicate. Imagine the fear they may experience coming to a workshop on teenage drug use or a panel discussion on adolescent suicide.

If we're willing to patiently work through the levels of this parent ministry approach, we'll have established a solid base of parental support long before we get to the level of educating parents when they tend to get squeamish. Gaining the trust of families is critical and, through a balanced approach to ministry, demonstrates that we're providing support and encouragement to everyone. A strong Parent Advisory Council can be an effective voice to parents, helping them understand the purpose and audience of the scheduled events. You can read more about how to establish such a group in Chapter 7.

• • •

Eight Obstacles to Parent Ministry

Review the eight obstacles to establishing a parent ministry. Discuss the questions with your youth ministry team, if you have one. Or ask a small group of trusted parents to consider them with you. If you have no context for discussion, take time for personal reflection.

Obstacles

1. Youth workers have to consider the needs of the whole youth group. Parents focus on their own kids.
2. Youth workers may know the inside scoop on family secrets.
3. Youth workers are too busy already and don't have time or energy for more programs.
4. Youth workers often love being needed. When we're insecure, we often shut parents out.
5. Parents may feel threatened when their kids seem drawn to the youth workers.
6. Parents may not respect young youth workers without teenagers of their own.
7. Parents may think they're hiring a baby-sitter.
8. Parents may experience a stigma associated with needing help.

Reflect and Discuss

1. What are the top three obstacles to a more effective ministry with parents in our setting?

2. What's the difference between ministry *to* parents and ministry *with* parents? Which are we trying to establish? How will parents sense the difference?

3. In what ways do we unconsciously shut out parents because of our need to be needed?

4. How can we communicate to parents that our role is more than providing entertainment for their kids?

5. What immediate steps can we take to begin building bridges of trust with parents?

Chapter 1

Assume Teens Have Parents

Acknowledge the Existence and Importance of Parents

"The intensity of emotion around even the most fundamental family issues has been divisive and discouraging to many."

"The picture of a parent—most often a father—is consistently used to help us understand God's nature."

The starting point for all effective parent ministry is to acknowledge the existence and importance of parents in the lives of all students. To *acknowledge* simply means to consciously admit a truth exists. The way most churches are programmed, we often don't see kids with their parents, so it's easy to forget that parents are part of the picture. We have to make a conscious effort to see kids as more than just members of our small group or confirmation class and to remember they're also members of a family.

We can get frustrated when we realize the first level of building a parent ministry is rooted in attitude, not action. We want to mix mortar and pile on bricks. But we don't establish solid family ministry by planning an event or teaching a Bible study. Instead, we create a solid foundation by getting the right perspective: seeing teens as sons and daughters and recognizing the inviolable link with family that is the primary force shaping their lives .

Acknowledge the Existence of Parents

Common sense and basic biology tell us that these kids who mysteriously appear in our youth rooms or in our study groups on cue each week must have come from somewhere. Unless we still buy the stork story, we know there must be a parent or two out there.

Because we are committed to relational ministry, we may see our relationships with our students as being the most important. (Notice the possessive language we use to reinforce *our* importance in the lives of *our* kids.) We look for ways to establish relationships with new students in our communities. We develop strategies for introducing the gospel into those relationships. We commit ourselves to being consistent, authentic, humble, teachable, and available in our relationships with them. Ministry is all about finding a way into the hearts of students so they can see Jesus in us. We pray for them and carefully monitor their friendships. We rejoice with them in their successes and weep with them in their disasters. We become what sociologists call *significant adults* in their lives. There's no question about it. We *are* important people to the kids in our care! **But we're not *the most* important people.**

We easily assume parents are diminishing in importance because of the natural adolescent tendency to talk about them in negative terms as they pull away to establish identities of their own. It's easy to see parents as incompetent, blundering buffoons if we listen to family stories told from the adolescent perspective. It's easy to forget that parents have been given the primary responsibility for the nurture and care of their children. But when we determine a ministry to parents is valid, we start by consciously acknowledging their existence.

Acknowledging parents means—

- We don't make decisions on behalf of kids without consulting their parents. We don't give advice contrary to advice given by a parent.

- We remain sensitive to the rhythms and realities of family life as we plan our programs and activities.

- We don't set ourselves up as surrogate parents even though our egos might enjoy the role.

- We look for ways to strengthen the bond between parent and child rather than allowing or promoting deterioration.

Exceptions to these practical principles are rare. In cases of genuinely dysfunctional families, certain moral and legal obligations factor in. (See **Ministry with Abusive, Unhealthy, or Highly Dysfunctional Parents** on page 163.) As a general rule of ministry, remember, teens have parents already!

Acknowledge the Importance of Parents

I usually love fireworks. It's great to sit back on a warm summer evening with the sky exploding and watch the reflected colors dancing on the water, but some of the wildest fireworks I've experienced haven't been the 4th of July variety. They've been generated in discussions around issues related to family definitions, family ministry, and family dynamics. I'll give you a recent personal example.

Our task seemed huge but manageable, given the incredible range of ministry experience that sat around the table that weekend. I was part of a national task force on family ministry. Our job was to get a nationwide perspective on the issues faced by families and then to assess strategies being implemented by various churches and ministries. Perhaps we could learn from one another.

The group of 10 was made up of people from a variety of ministry settings and denominational perspectives, but we held our faith in common so it felt like we had a comfortable starting point. The chair led us through the customary *hi-how-are-ya's* and then pointed us to the first of a dozen agenda items that would guide us through the two days we had to work together. It was a 30-minute introductory item identified innocently enough as Defining the Family. You can probably guess the end of the story. After two full days on Item 1, we were no closer to consensus than when we had begun, and we had seen a fireworks show or two unlike what any of us could have anticipated. We couldn't even agree on what a family was, much less how to meet its needs.

The intensity of emotion around even the most fundamental family issues has been divisive and discouraging to many who have thought about family ministry. Theology, politics, and pragmatics all play a part. A lot is at stake and everyone seems committed to promoting his or her own perspective. However, in spite of all the passion and the apparent lack of agreement, we have some good reasons to preserve, strengthen, and support the family in any way we can.

Recognizing those reasons gives us a solid foundation for building a ministry to parents that strengthens their hand and equips them for ministry to their own kids. Here are three solid, biblically based benefits that accrue when we do all we can to strengthen the role of parents in the lives of their children.

A wise parent coaches children in basic life and relational skills.

Most social scientists agree that one of the primary functions of the family is to socialize children into the culture they're born into. This simply means to teach them the values, traditions, norms, and mores expected of healthy, productive adults. Much of this learning is solidified during the teenage years. Adolescence is an ideal time to develop the critical skills of interpersonal communication, conflict resolution, emotional management, collaboration, responding to authority, and mutual respect and consideration, to mention a few. The committed, safe, and loving context of a healthy family is an ideal place to learn and practice these skills. Sadly, just about the time these lessons can be implemented, some families are beginning to come apart.

The fact is that, for better or worse, children learn their most important lessons about life and relationships from watching their parents. The haunting lyrics of "Cats in the Cradle," recorded by Harry Chapin, remind us that when it comes to family relationships, our children often grow up just like us: Through the years, a father is too busy to spend much time with his son. He makes hollow promises about the future. By the time the father wants to spend time with his son, the boy is busy with his own life, making promises about spending time together in the future. Unhealthy, dysfunctional patterns of communication are just as contagious as healthy ones.

The assumption that parents coach children in basic life and relational skills is beautifully illustrated in Scripture. Paul makes a profound point to the rookie pastor Timothy in 1 Timothy 5:1-2. He uses Timothy's family context as the framework for helping him understand the ins and outs of healthy adult relationships, in this case, the relationships Timothy has with members of his congregation. Paul basically says, "Listen, Timothy. If you're not sure how to treat the older men in your church just think of them as though they were your dad. When you're relating to the younger guys, think of them as your brothers. Older women should be treated as if they're your mom, and the younger women should be treated with the purity your sister deserves."

What Paul assumes (and other passages indicate he knew Timothy's family) is that young Tim had learned the important skills of human relationships in his own home. Apparently he had the kind of rapport with his mom and dad that gave him a model for how to treat older people in his church. His relationship with his siblings must have been such that the lessons learned could be applied in adult life.

When we live with an emerging generation that struggles to respond appropriately to authority and often struggles with basic community-living skills and when we see young adults who struggle with interpersonal communication, conflict resolution, and cooperation, we need to ask ourselves if perhaps they haven't had a good practice field on which to learn those skills.

The family isn't the only place such skills can be learned, but it can be the best place, especially for adolescents and parents who understand the value of family relationships. Healthy families mean that a lot less remedial work and relational damage control will be necessary later in life. That's an investment worth making.

An involved parent passes faith from one generation to the next.

Christianity is just one short generation from extinction. That's a point worth noting, but don't be overly alarmed. Frankly, it's always been that way. Each emerging generation since the beginning of time has had the same choice: to embrace the good news of the gospel or to ignore it. The challenge has been to find effective ways to communicate the good news to the next generation.

Faith lived out transparently and expressed authentically has a drawing power more potent than sermons and lectures. Jesus said our faith would be authenticated in our relationships with one another. "By this all men will know that you are my disciples, if you love one another" (John 13:35). The family context is a natural place for love to happen. A parent's godly life can be a profoundly effective means of demonstrating the reality of the gospel. Children are able to see faith applied in every circumstance of life. The closeness of family means that we see one another at our best and at our worst. Faith that takes root in the honest reality of family life has great potential to grow healthy and strong.

The fundamental principle that puts the responsibility for the spiritual formation of children into the hands of parents is firmly rooted in Scripture. When Moses called on parents in Deuteronomy 6 to impress God's commandments on their children, he described what that would look like in real life. He says, "Talk about them when you sit at home and when you walk along the road, when you lie down and when you get up. Tie them as symbols on your hands and bind them on your foreheads. Write them on the doorframes of your houses and on your gates" (Deut 6:7-9). What Moses is saying to parents is to help children encounter faith in every life circumstance.

What a tragedy when just a few decades later "another generation grew up, who knew neither the Lord nor what he had done for Israel" (Judges 2:10). Evidently the generation who, under Joshua's leadership, had seen God do one miracle after another had not communicated their faith to the next generation. The following years are some of the darkest in the spiritual lives of God's people. Examples of parents dropping the ball with their children's faith development can be seen repeatedly in biblical narratives: Eli and his sons, Solomon and Rehoboam, and David and Amnon to name a few.

A family-based ministry that sees parents as the primary

Parents are the primary Christian educators in the church, and the family is the God-ordained institution for faith-building in children and youth and for the passing of faith from one generation to the next.

Ben Freudenburg, *The Family Friendly Church* (Group, 1998), page 21

spiritual nurturers of their own children could be the most effective evangelism and discipleship program ever devised. Unfortunately the opposite is also true. Nothing is more crippling to a child's faith than seeing the hypocrisy of a parent who consistently fails to walk the talk while pretending everything is okay.

God calls people into relationship with himself in a variety of ways; godly parents aren't the only means by which a young person can embrace faith and grow in it, but it's as good a way as I know. A youth worker who understands the importance of equipping parents to participate in the spiritual journeys of their own children will be facilitating a process that acknowledges God's heart for the family.

A loving parent is a powerful portrait of God.

Perhaps the strongest case for investing in parents and families has to do with how God presents himself to us. The Bible is full of metaphors that help our finite minds grasp spiritual mysteries. God himself is one of those mysteries. The picture of a parent—most often a father—is consistently used to help us understand his nature.

The Psalmist calls God a "father to the fatherless" (Psalm 68:5). Dr. Luke talks about his consistent and generous provision for his children (Luke 11:11-3). Paul tells us that we have such an intimate relationship with our heavenly father that we call him Abba—Dad (Romans 8:14-17). The writer to the Hebrews helps us understand God's discipline by using the picture of an earthly father (Hebrews 12:6-11).

Unfortunately, for many teenagers the image of parents has become twisted and distorted. I was recently praying with a student after a lengthy conversation together. She had expressed deep concerns about her relationship with God. She simply didn't know if he could be trusted. I began my prayer, as I often do, with the address, "Dear heavenly Father." I sensed her stiffen as I said the words. Through angrily clenched teeth she interrupted me with the contemptuous words, "You can call him anything, but don't call him *father.*" Her picture of a father was negative, unloving, abusive, and distant.

And yet, something in the soul of every human being longs to experience a relationship with a strong and gentle father. **As families continue to flounder and as fathers abdicate their roles in the lives of their children the rich imagery of the Bible has potential to lose its impact.**

The Bible consistently reinforces the notion that the family is worth investing in and parents are worth supporting. Family provides a place for kids to learn life's important relational skills. Parents nurture their children spiritually and point them to an authentic growing faith. And parents can provide a taste of what our heavenly father is like by being a reflection of his character—God "with skin on."

Acknowledge the Growing Complexity of Parenting Arrangements

One more important area must be acknowledged in ministry with parents: the growing complexity of family systems. Maybe you've seen a wedding photo shoot that reminds you of this reality: "Okay, why don't we get a shot with the bride and groom with her mom and step-dad on the right and his dad and step-mom on the left. Good. Now if we could have the bride's children sitting on the grass in front of her and the groom's daughter and her partner come in on the left side as well…" You've got the picture. The days of mom and dad with 2.3 kids and a cocker spaniel are long gone. We can't assume anything about the structure of a family group.

This would seem like an appropriate place to insert a page or two of depressing statistics on recent changes in the family, but if you've been in youth ministry more than a few weeks, you can see the impact of family restructuring in your own group's kids. We can count on a couple of truths when it comes to the changing shape of the family.

Changing family configurations is a growing phenomenon. Plenty of students in our care will be living in nontraditional family systems, including single parent homes headed by either a father or a mother, step- and blended families, all sorts of shared custodial arrangements, foster care, group homes, and extended family (aunt, uncle, sibling, grandparent to name the most common). Lots of teenagers don't live with their biological mom, dad, and siblings under the same roof.

Family restructuring makes a difference. With very few exceptions (some researchers would say no exceptions), parents and children are profoundly affected when a family breaks up and is recognized in a new form. In most cases the impact is negative. The purpose of this book is not to deal with the question of divorce and its impact or the challenges of growing up in a single parent home or the pros and cons of blending families. Other resources deal adequately with these issues. It's enough here to remind youth workers that ministry to parents must take into account the realities of the changing family shape in current days.

Chapter 10 deals more specifically with the practical ministry implications of family variations. General principles of ministry we all need to be reminded of include—

- Be sensitive to the extra challenges faced by parents in restructured family systems.

- Be careful in your use of language (for example, referring to parents as couples).

- Beware of jumping to conclusions until you know the whole story.

- Be particularly supportive of parents *and* kids in single parent situations. They have unique challenges.

One final word: it's not all bad news. In spite of the lack of strength and stability we often see in families around us, plenty of healthy homes exist. Support and celebrate them as well. These families are far from perfect, but they are authentic relational communities where the growth of each individual is a priority.

Until we've consciously acknowledged the existence, importance, and complexity of the families we work with, we have no basis for a ministry to them. **Parents are the key players in the lives of their teenagers.** Equipping them for their role is a responsibility youth workers are well positioned to do. An investment in a parent will pay dividends in the lives of their kids.

• • •

Chapter 2

Three Cheers for Moms and Dads!

Affirm Parents and the Family

"Cultural voices belittle the institution of marriage, predicting the death of family and trivializing the place of parents."

"To hear someone they respect speak positively about their parents is a surprise."

(Pyramid graphic: CO-NURTURE 9, EDUCATE 8, INVOLVE 7, EQUIP 6, CONNECT 5, ENCOURAGE 4, COMMUNICATE 3, **AFFIRM 2**, ACKNOWLEDGE 1)

Now that we've acknowledged the existence and importance of parents in the lives of their kids, it's time to get proactive about parent ministry. But don't get your programming machinery revved up yet. We're still not ready to schedule events and plan activities. Remember that parent ministry is based on mutual respect and shared trust. Keep in mind also, that our ultimate goal is to be partners with parents, co-nurturers of the adolescents we share a love for. That kind of a relationship doesn't happen overnight, especially in light of some of the natural obstacles we've reviewed (pages 6-11) that are often detrimental to partnerships.

The second level for building a parent ministry is to affirm parents whenever we have—or make—the opportunity. **We consciously and visibly** demonstrate **the respect and regard we have for them as the primary nurturers of their children.** When we affirm parents we validate their role and give them credibility in the eyes of their teens. As significant adults in the lives of adolescents, youth workers have the opportunity to be a positive voice for parents and the family. Teenagers need to hear positive messages about parents, whenever possible, since many feel skeptical about the value of these "old people" at this stage in their developmental journey—at least part of the time.

When you're focusing on the affirmation level, think of yourself as a public relations agent for the parents you serve. (By the way, P.R. can also stand for *Parents Rule!*) Affirming parents means—

- We are conscious to speak positively about the parent-teen relationship.

- We defend parents when their kids are trashing them.

- We take care not to belittle parents or reinforce negative images kids may have, which undermines parent-teen relationships.

Affirming parents is tougher than it sounds. I was recently reminded of how easily fuel can be added to the fire through careless words when I was driving a car full of teenagers to play laser tag. As we headed onto the highway I popped some edgy music into my stereo. When the first chords filled the car, I heard the approving murmur of all the kids. I looked in the rearview mirror and over the noise said, "Your parents would hate this music wouldn't they?" It sounded innocent enough, but what was I *really* saying? "Your parents are dorks. I'm cool. Who needs parents when you've got me?"

In this chapter we'll consider ways you can make parents look good to their kids. You'll find that the little things you do to cast the family in a positive light can go a long way in shaping the attitudes kids have toward their parents. And when kids feel positive about parents, parents are much more likely to get involved.

Why Parents Need Affirmation

Teenagers generally have a love-hate relationship with their parents. They're trying to detach themselves from their families and establish identities of their own, and yet, deep down they desire ongoing involvement from their parents. Anthony Wolf captured the tension in the title of his practical book on parenting adolescents: *Get Out of My Life, but First Could You Drive Me and Cheryl to the Mall?* (Noonday Press, 1992). This ambivalence is often the root of the intense conflict that develops between kids and their parents during the adolescent years. In their emotional immaturity adolescents often lash out at parents and react irrationally to minor differences of perspective. Parents, fearing a loss of relationship either withdraw or tighten controls and the relational tug-of-war begins.

As youth workers we wander into the battle zone and immediately feel the pressure to pick sides. When we join with kids against their parents or with parents against their kids, we simply intensify the conflict. It's important for us to find an approach that helps diffuse tension rather than increasing it.

Affirming parents diffuses tension. Instead of being *against* anyone we are simply speaking *for* parents—just like we often speak *for* kids when we're encouraging parents. **By placing our emphasis on strengthening the relationship instead of on undermining one side or the other, we bring stability to an otherwise volatile situation.**

We have one more reason to be a positive voice for parents and the family: many of the students we work with don't have the luxury of strong role models when it comes to marriage, parenting, and the family. In fact plenty of cultural voices belittle the institution of marriage, predicting the death of family and trivializing the place of parents in the lives of their kids. Whenever we speak positively about family, we're communicating its importance to a new generation. Shaping healthy, positive attitudes is always significant work!

Ideas for Affirming Parents

A Lot of Little Things
Affirming parents doesn't need to happen through complex programs and scheduled events. Communicate a new attitude about parents to kids on a day-to-day basis. When teens see us responding positively to parents and treating them with value in our everyday encounters with them, they gradually will adjust their perspective. We simply need to look for consistent, little ways to communicate the importance of parents. With some practice these affirmations can become second nature.

- Let kids know you're anxious to meet their parents. After you've been introduced (or introduced yourself) and when you get a few minutes alone with the student, say something positive about the encounter:

— Your parents seem like they're a lot of fun.
— Your mom sure is proud of you.
— That's a very cool pocket protector your dad was wearing.

- When kids ask you for advice, get in the habit of asking, "How do you suppose your parents might feel about it?" Or after giving them your thoughts on the question say, "Those are my ideas, but you should ask your mom what she thinks, too."

- Find positive comments to make about students' parents. Do it in the presence of their friends whenever possible.

  — Your dad does such a great job of coaching his team. The kids sure seem to love him.
  — Your mom's solo was great this morning. No wonder you guys are all so musical.
  — Your dad sure puts a lot of work into teaching his class each week.
  — Your mom has such a welcoming way with people.

  Many kids haven't thought about their parents as anything but out of touch. To hear someone they respect speak positively is a nice surprise.

- Thank parents publicly for their investment in their children.

- Pray for parents during your times with students.

- Once you're ready to involve parents, encourage them to use their gifts. Let kids feel pride in their parents' contributions.

Teaching Applications with a Parental Spin

The teaching component of a youth worker's job is strengthened when young people are helped to find ways to take the principles of scripture into their world and apply the truth there. Most published curriculum comes with well-written applications for each lesson. "Here's how you can put this truth into action at your school...with your friends...in our youth group..."

Recently I evaluated a number of current Sunday School curriculum and Bible lessons and found that in most hardly a mention is made of how truth might apply to family relationships. The applications were creative, appropriate, and meaningful but apparently oblivious to the parent-teen relationship. I'm not suggesting that every time we open the scripture with kids we ought to end up talking about home. However, as we personalize our teaching material, we do well to ask ourselves whether a natural application to parents or family can be made. If so, make the connection.

Welcome to Our World

In the fall when church programs are getting started for the new school year, **have the youth ministry department host a brief ceremony during the church service commissioning first-time parents of teens.** The ritual can be as simple or elaborate as you like, but it's nice to invite the rookie parents up front and have all parents of teens stand as you offer a prayer of dedication. Avoid prayers that sound like this will be an impossible mountain to climb and anyone who makes it through is fortunate. The focus of the prayer can be on the joy and privilege of parenting young people who are moving toward adulthood and a celebration of good things to come. You might present parents with an appropriate book like *Cleared for*

Takeoff by Wayne Rice or *Understanding Today's Youth Culture* by Walt Mueller. If you want to have some fun with the gifts, you can present T-shirts that say, *I feel lucky! My kid just turned 13!*

Parent Prayer Time

Offer a guided prayer exercise that encourages kids to pray for their parents in various areas of their lives. Have kids bow their heads and think for a few moments about their parents. Say something like—

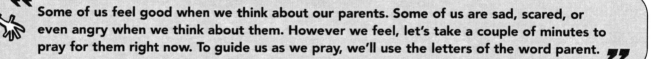

Some of us feel good when we think about our parents. Some of us are sad, scared, or even angry when we think about them. However we feel, let's take a couple of minutes to pray for them right now. To guide us as we pray, we'll use the letters of the word parent.

Depending on the family situations of your students, you may need to acknowledge adoptive parents, foster parents, or relatives handling the parenting role. Think through the possibility of helping your students pray for both their biological parents and their adoptive parents or guardians. Guide your students through the prayer with the following cues:

Pressure
Identify a pressure your mom or dad is experiencing currently. It could be money pressure, job pressure, maybe something related to their health or a tough decision he or she has to make. Pray that God will give them his strength to deal with the pressure and for your parent to grow spiritually because of it.

Attitude
Think of an attitude you have toward your parents that could use an adjustment. Tell God what the attitude is and ask him for help in changing it.

Relationship
Your parents are in lots of relationships—with friends, with family members, with neighbors, with each other, and with you. Think about a relationship they have that could use some prayer right now. Ask God to help them act with grace and forgiveness. If nothing else comes to mind, ask the Lord for his wisdom as they parent you.

Emotions
Has your mom or dad shown any of these emotions lately: sadness, fear, anger, worry, loneliness, helplessness? Ask the Lord to bring hope, understanding, and healing to your parent.

Needs
Think about something your mom or dad needs—maybe a job, healing, a friend, rest, wisdom for a decision, encouragement in some challenge. Ask God to meet your parent's need.

Thanks
Say thanks to God for your imperfect parents. You can thank him for sacrifices they have made for you, for the life experiences they've had that have affected them, or for boundaries they've set that have kept you safe. Then think of a way you can say thanks to them yourself.

• • •

Raising Parents You Can Live With

A teen meeting to affirm parents and promote communication with them

The *Big* Picture

Kids often make the assumption that parents are fully responsible for the quality (or lack of quality) of the relationships in their family. This lesson shows teenagers that they can take responsibility for part of the relationship and make an investment in a healthier family.

Bible Basis

1 Corinthians 13:4-8

Family Farm

You'll need...

- **Family Farm Fun** (page 28), one copy
- **Animal Moms, Animal Dads, Animal Babies,** and **Animal Families** (pages 29-32), one copy of each page on a different color
- Tape or push pins

OR

- Copies of **Family Farm Matching Quiz** (page 33), one for each group
- Pencils

For an active opener, copy Family Farm Fun on page 28. Cut the names apart, and post them on the wall around the room. Copy **Animal Moms, Animal Dads, Animal Babies, and Animal Families** (pages 29-32) on four different colors of paper (one color per category), and cut the names apart. As students arrive, randomly give them several words. Let students stick the names by the appropriate cards posted around the room.

For a less mobile option, let students divide into groups of two or three. Give each group a copy of the **Family Farm Matching Quiz** (page 33). Direct students to match the moms, dads, babies, and families with the type of animal they represent.

Review the results. Make a transition to your lesson by saying something like—

The world is full of families—moms, dads, and kids. Today we want to talk about your family and how you can help make it better. Let's start by talking about parents.

Fathers Fuming, Mothers Moaning

You'll need...
- Butcher paper
- Tape or push pins
- Markers

Create a graffiti wall by posting butcher paper at eye level. Provide lots of markers. Write *Fathers Fuming and Mothers Moaning* at the top. Kickstart the exercise by having a few parent peeves already scattered on the paper.

- Your room looks like a bomb went off in there.
- Your friends! Where do you find these people?
- Your curfew was an hour ago.

As kids arrive, hand them a marker or crayon and let them add fuming and moaning they've heard.

After a few minutes, or when a good collection of statements has been written, stop them and have them step back from the wall. Take a marker of a different color and say something like—

Whose fault is it that parents are upset about all this stuff? Some of it will be an over-reaction on their part, and some of it will just be bad choices or irresponsibility on our part. Let's establish percentages on some of these. Let's start with the messy room. How much of the problem is legitimately our fault, and how much is an over-reaction? Sixty percent our fault, 40 percent over-reaction? Or is it more like 80-20?

Look at several of the categories and have them discuss the breakdowns. Write down the percentages they settle on.

Transition to the lesson by saying something along this line—

It looks like we all need to take at least some responsibility for the tension we feel at home. During this lesson we want to look at ways we can work together at solutions.

Prime-Time Parents

You'll need...
- **Prime-Time Parents** (page 34), one copy per pair
- Pencils

Get your students into pairs and give them **Prime-Time Parents** (page 34) and a pencil. Tell them they have two minutes to brainstorm 10 television or movie moms and dads and write them on the television screens. They can use only one parent from each show or movie. They can write the character's name (Tim the Tool Man) or the actor's name *and* the name of the show (Tim Allen, *Home Improvement*).

After students have generated their lists, have them write down one good-parent characteristic for each person. A simple adjective or short phrase will do (loves his kid, listens without interrupting). No repeats. All the characteristics on their list should be different. Kids will have a list of 10 positive characteristics of parents.

Have pairs get together to form groups of four. From the two lists, have students generate a top-10 list of qualities.

The Perfect Parent

You'll need...
- **Mah-vah-las Mom, Dy-no-mite Dad** (page 35), one copy per group
- Pencils

Cut up a copy of **Mah-vah-las Mom, Dy-no-mite Dad** (page 35), one for each group of four you're working with. Have your students arrange the traits from most important to least important. Or have students place the cards into three categories: Gotta Have It, Would Be Nice, or No Big Deal. Students can add qualities on the blank cards.

The purpose of the activity is to get kids to identify the parental qualities that matter to them and those that are less important. If you're working with more than four discussion groups, combine pairs of groups together to share their lists and the reasons why they've ranked the qualities as they have. If you have two or three discussion groups, post the lists at the front of the room. Let your teens explain their lists and reasons.

Wrap up the exercise by discussing the following question:

> **How would your family relationships be different if your parents always displayed the Gotta Have It (or five most important) characteristics?**

What's Love Got to Do with It?

You'll need...
- **L-O-V-E,** (page 36), copied and cut apart, one card per student (optional)
- **House of Love** (page 37), one copy per group
- Pencils

Form new groups of four by handing out cards marked with the letters L, O, V, and E on them and having students find people with the other letters needed to form the word *love*. Or you can simply ask students to get together with people they haven't been grouped with for previous activities.

Say something like—

> **When you hear the word *love* what do you think of? Maybe pictures of candlelight dinners or a bouquet of roses. Romantic love is a nice concept, but what happens when all that**

Continued on next page...

... Continued

romance results in a family? Love isn't quite as easy when you think about loving your parents or your brothers and sisters. Where's the love when the candles have gone out and you're trying to make your family work? Parents are supposed to love their kids, and kids are supposed to love their parents, but what does that look like in a real family like yours?

We're going to look at a section of the Bible that often gets read at weddings—but there's no reason to believe that's what Paul had in mind when he wrote it. In fact if we look at the letter it came from we'll see that it was written to a group of people who weren't getting along very well at all. They couldn't seem to agree on anything. They were blaming each other whenever anything went wrong. Some of them were downright selfish and out of control. Does that sound like home? 🙶

Give each student a copy of **House of Love** (page 37). You'll find the Scripture, 1 Corinthians 13:4-7, printed out for reference. Have students work in their groups to form two lists: *what love is and does and what love isn't and doesn't do.* The lists will look something like these—

What love is and does
- Is patient
- Is kind
- Keeps no record of wrongs
- Rejoices with truth
- Always protects
- Always trusts
- Always hopes
- Always perseveres

What love isn't and doesn't do
- Does not envy
- Does not boast
- Is not proud
- Is not rude
- Is not self-seeking
- Is not easily angered
- Does not delight in evil
- Does not fail

Once the groups complete their lists, have them circle four characteristics of love parents often have trouble with and star four characteristics kids often have trouble with.

Next have each group pick one circled characteristic (parent problem) and one starred characteristic (teen problem). Give students five to 10 minutes to write and rehearse a short conversation between two or more people showing how people might collide in a real-life situation without those characteristics. Let each group perform its sketch.

For some students, parental violations of love may be severe. The incest victim who reads "love always protects" and the boy beaten by his father who reads "love is not easily angered" know their experiences are inconsistent with the Bible's definition of love.

Acknowledge to your students that, if these experiences are theirs, they are not the cause of nor responsible for the choices their parents make. The pain they feel is real. Let your teens know you are available to listen and to help. (You are probably a legally mandated reporter. Know your responsibilities toward abused students.)

The lesson applications will be difficult for abused teens to implement.

Turn the Tables

Say something like—

> **We can't do anything here to force our parents to change, but maybe over time we can make our relationships better. Pick one area that one of your parents has trouble with...patience, trust, anger...whichever quality from 1 Corinthians that you want to focus on.**
>
> **Think of one thing *you* can do to make it easier for your parent to be more loving in that area. Fill in the sentence at the bottom of the handout. Find a partner and read your sentences to one another. Make a plan to check on each other to be sure you're following through.**

Closing

Have students pick one characteristic of love that *they* find tough to apply with a parent. On the back of **House of Love**, have the kids write a prayer telling God about their difficulty and asking him for help. Encourage students to be specific about the kind of help they want.

Family Farm Fun

(see page 23)

Copy this page and cut apart the animal names. Post them around the room. Use with **Animal Moms, Animal Dads, Animal Babies,** and **Animal Families** on pages 29-32.

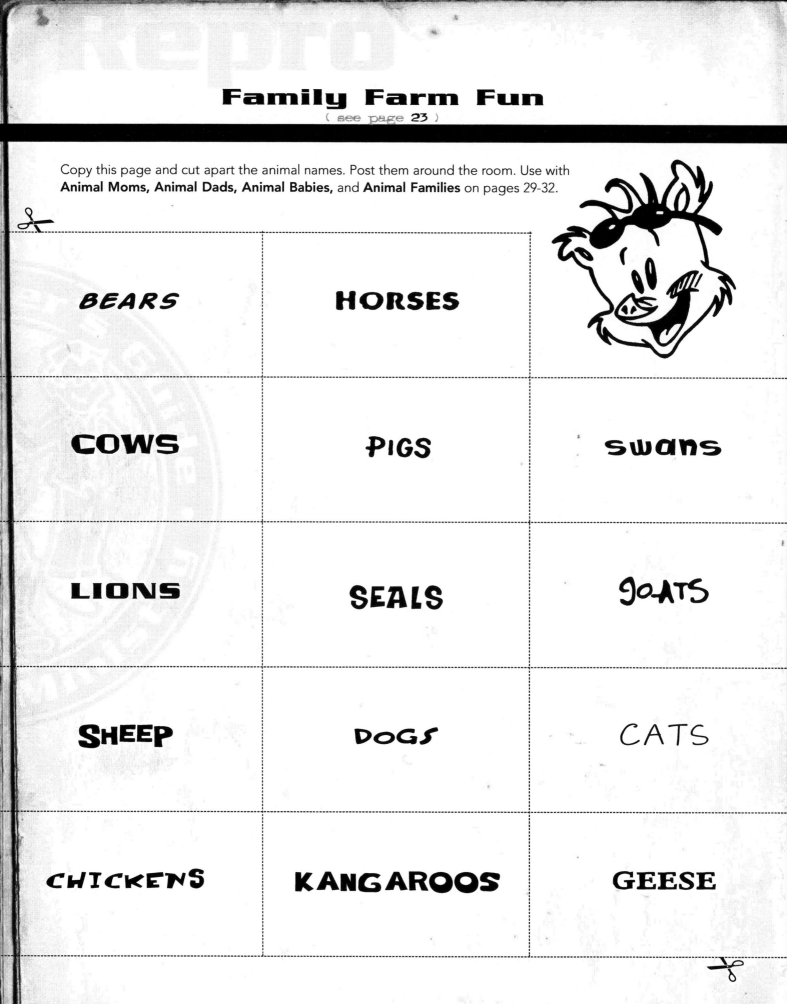

BEARS	HORSES	
COWS	PIGS	swans
LIONS	SEALS	goats
SHEEP	DOGS	CATS
CHICKENS	KANGAROOS	GEESE

Animal Moms

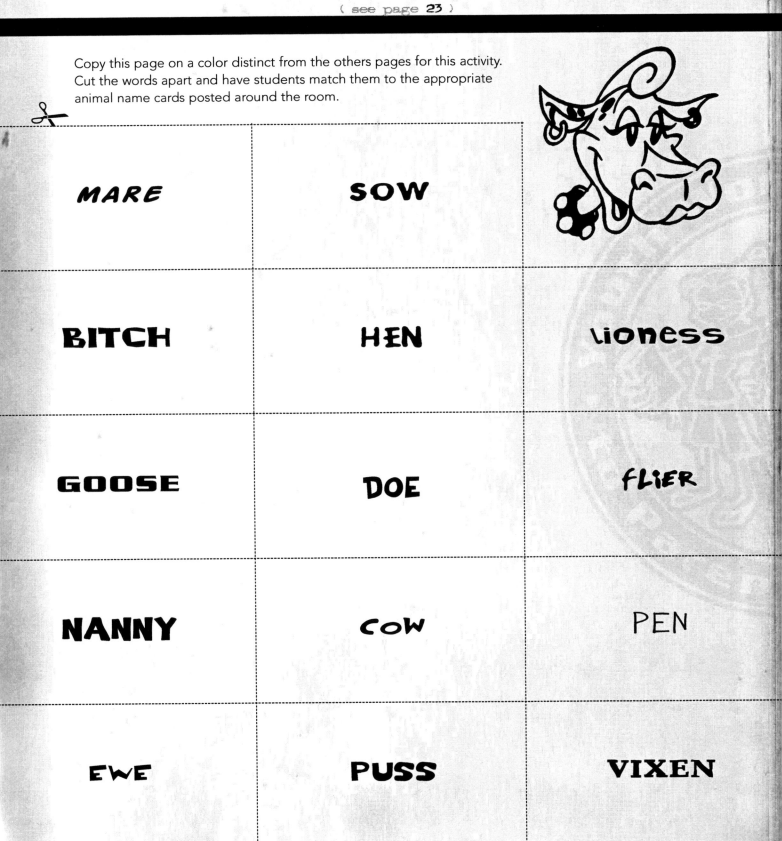

(see page 23)

Copy this page on a color distinct from the others pages for this activity.
Cut the words apart and have students match them to the appropriate
animal name cards posted around the room.

MARE	SOW	
BITCH	HEN	Lioness
GOOSE	DOE	FLiER
NANNY	COW	PEN
EWE	PUSS	VIXEN

Animal Dads

(see page 23)

Copy this page on a color distinct from the others pages for this activity. Cut the words apart and have students match them to the appropriate animal name cards posted around the room.

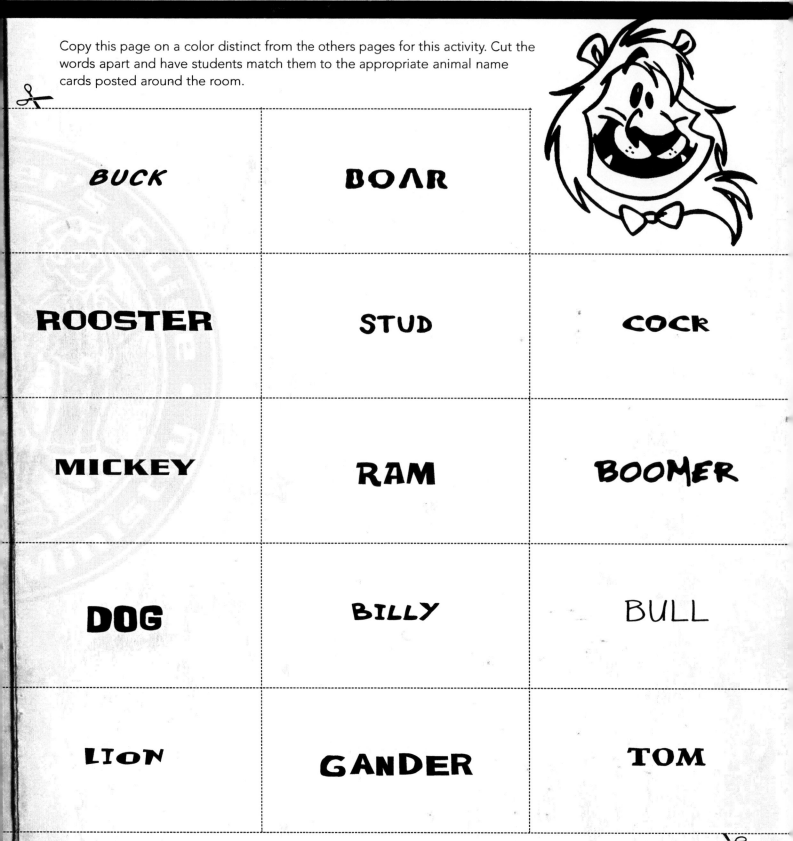

BUCK	BOAR	
ROOSTER	STUD	COCK
MICKEY	RAM	BOOMER
DOG	BILLY	BULL
LION	GANDER	TOM

Animal Babies

(see page 23)

Copy this page on a color distinct from the others pages for this activity.
Cut the words apart and have students match them to the appropriate
animal name cards posted around the room.

GOSLING	JOEY	
FARROW	CUB	Chick
KID	FOAL	PUPPY
WHELP	KITTEN	LAMB
FAWN	CALF	CYGNET

Animal Families

(see page 23)

Copy this page on a color distinct from the others pages for this activity. Cut the words apart and have students match them to the appropriate animal name cards posted around the room.

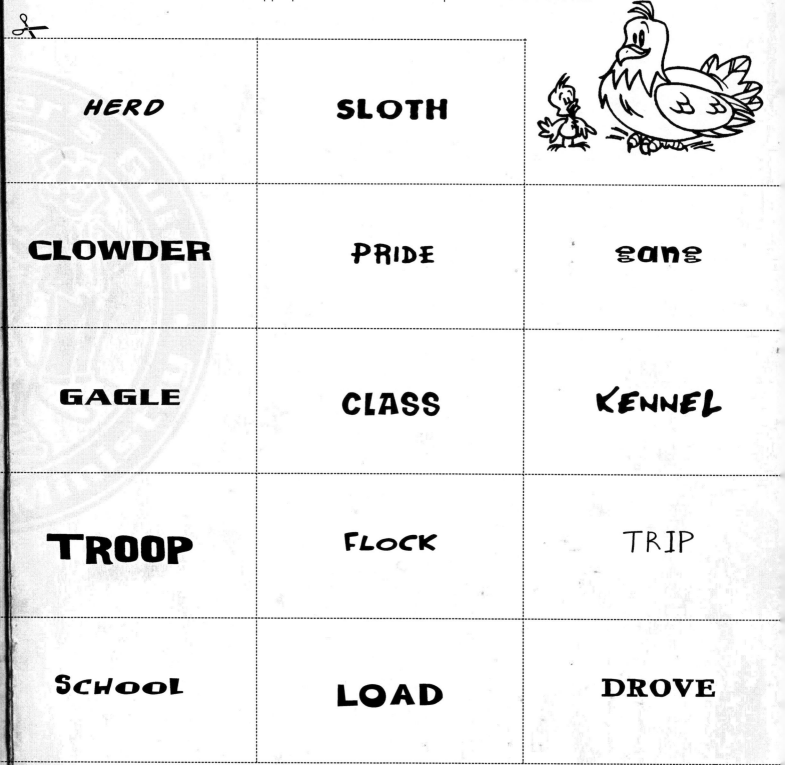

HERD	SLOTH	
CLOWDER	PRIDE	BAND
GAGLE	CLASS	KENNEL
TROOP	FLOCK	TRIP
SCHOOL	LOAD	DROVE

Family Farm Matching Quiz

(see page 23)

Draw lines connecting the animal names in the middle column to the matching names for mothers, fathers, babies, and families. Some names might be used more than once, some not at all.

The mother is called a...	The father is called a...	The Animal Name...	The baby is called...	A family is called...
MARE	BUCK	**bears**	GOSLING	HERD
SOW	BOAR	**horses**	JOEY	SLOTH
VIXEN	TOM	**geese**	CYGNET	DROVE
BITCH	ROOSTER	**cows**	FARROW	CLOWDER
HEN	STUD	**pigs**	CUB	PRIDE
LIONESS	COCK	**swans**	CHICK	GANG
GOOSE	MICKEY	**lions**	KID	GAGGLE
DOE	RAM	**seals**	FOAL	CLASS
FLIER	BOOMER	**goats**	PUPPY	KENNEL
NANNY	DOG	**sheep**	WHELP	TROOP
COW	BILLY	**dogs**	KITTEN	FLOCK
PEN	BULL	**cats**	LAMB	TRIP
EWE	LION	**chickens**	FAWN	SCHOOL
PUSS	GANDER	**kangaroos**	CALF	LOAD

Prime-Time Parents

(see page 24)

Brainstorm the names of 10 television or movie moms and dads. Write them on the television screens. You can use only one parent from each show or movie. You can write the character's name or the actor's name *and* the name of the show.

Then write one good-parent characteristic for each person. A simple adjective or short phrase will do (loves his kid, listens without interrupting). No repeats. All the characteristics on your list should be different.

Mah-vah-las Mom, Dy-no-mite Dad

(see page 25)

Cut apart the following parent traits. Have your students arrange the traits from most important to least important. Or have students place the traits into three categories: Gotta Have It, Would Be Nice, or No Big Deal. Students can add qualities on the blank cards.

GOOD LISTENER	CALM WHEN DISCUSSING ISSUES
NON-JUDGMENTAL	GOOD MONEY MANAGER
LIKES LOUD MUSIC	LIKES MY FRIENDS
AFFECTIONATE	STRONG SPIRITUAL LEADER
SHARP DRESSER	YOUTHFUL
SENSE OF HUMOR	PHYSICALLY FIT
ATTRACTIVE	WILLING TO APPOLOGIZE

Cut the letters apart and give each student one letter. Students form groups according to the letters they are holding.

✁

L	O	V	E
L	O	V	E
L	O	V	E
L	O	V	e
L	O	V	E
L	O	V	E

House of Love
(see page 26)

Love is patient, love is kind. It does not envy, it does not boast, it is not proud. It is not rude, it is not self-seeking, it is not easily angered, it keeps no record of wrongs. Love does not delight in evil but rejoices with the truth. It always protects, always trusts, always hopes, always perseveres. Love never fails.

—1 Corinthians 13:4-8

1. Make a list of love's characteristics mentioned in 1 Corinthians 13.

What Love Is and Does   *What Love Isn't and Doesn't Do*

2. Circle four characteristics in your lists that parents have trouble with. Draw stars by four characteristics teens have trouble with.

3. With your group, pick one circled and one starred characteristic. Write a short sketch between two or more people, showing how an encounter might look in a real-life situation without those characteristics.

4. Think about the following sentence. Fill in the blanks with your answers:

ONE CHARACTERISTIC OF LOVE THAT CHALLENGES MY _____ **IS**
_____ (mom/dad)

_____ **. I COULD MAKE IT EASIER FOR** _____
_____ (her/him)

IF I _____ **.**

Chapter 3

Communication is a Two-Way Street

Communicate Clearly and Listen Carefully to Parents

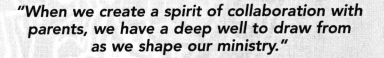

"When we create a spirit of collaboration with parents, we have a deep well to draw from as we shape our ministry."

"When I meet the 'parent' from hell, I'm often amazed at how emotionally healthy and mentally balanced that parent turns out to be."

"We'll be playing hide-and-seek in the freezer at the meat packing plant."

If we believe that parents are responsible for the care and protection of their children, we will take our responsibility of communicating with them seriously. We've acknowledged their existence and importance, and we're doing all we can to make them look good to their kids. Now it's time to focus on connecting with them. **Parents always appreciate being in the information loop when it comes to ministry priorities, scheduling, financial arrangements, leadership, and other practical details.** As youth workers we aren't operating in isolation from parents—in fact we should actually see ourselves as being accountable to parents in the ministry we provide for their kids.

Communication is not just telling; communication also involves listening. It's a two-way process. In this chapter we'll take our ministry with parents one step further by considering how we can be a voice *and* ears for the parents we serve. We'll find that both components are equally important and pay solid dividends in our relationships with moms and dads.

Why Parents Need to Be Consulted and Informed

R-E-S-P-E-C-T!

Soliciting feedback and keeping parents thoroughly informed about the details is the simplest and most effective way to express our respect for them. It's our way of saying, "You're in charge of your kids. I'm here to serve your family. Here's what you need to know about what's going on in the youth group part of your life. How can we work together?"

Communication Breakdown

Don't assume that any piece of information you entrust to an adolescent will ever arrive at home. It's more likely that parents will find out about a planned barbecue from rumors circulating in the church foyer than from the printed invitations that were sent home.

It's a grim reality. If we want parents to know what's going on, we need to find ways to tell them ourselves. Even when we give students information on paper to take home, chances are best that the flier will end up as lint in the dryer.

If a teenager does make an attempt to convey the message, information will be wrong or missing on three of four points. Parents may find out a retreat is coming up, but they have no idea where or when, who it's for, or how much it will cost.

Bin Dair, Dun Dat

Most of us are working with parents who are older and wiser than we are. Their experience is an invaluable resource for us to tap into. Many of them will know the history of your group, church, or community in ways that we don't. Perhaps they have important information on individuals who we may be considering for leadership. Parents have gained some wisdom, even in their short few years of raising adolescents. When we create a spirit of collaboration with parents, we will have a deep well to draw from as we shape our ministry.

We Need All the Friends We Can Get

An informed parent can be our strongest ally…our ears, eyes, and voices. Moms and dads typically hang out with other moms and dads, and one of the favorite topics of conversation is their kids. Inevitably some parent will have a twisted perspective on something that is happening in the youth ministry or some inaccurate information about an activity or an unfounded opinion about someone or something. When we can't be there to defend ourselves, it's comforting to know that we've got friends out there who are on our team.

Hold Me...Accountable

The nature of youth ministry may mean limited accountability when it comes to the use of our time and energy. Much of our ministry takes place in the car, in the mall, or at the football field. We may not spend much time in our offices. We don't fit well into the clock-punching 9-to-5 routine that some jobs are built on. We can easily become lazy and unfocussed.

Although we may not always appreciate it, parents are perhaps in the best position to be our—sometimes self-appointed—accountability partners. If we constantly communicate a listening and teachable spirit, they can help us with our ministry effectiveness.

(I know. I know. Some parents will always be whining and never understand the out-of-office nature of our work, but feedback from the others is invaluable.)

Just the Facts, Ma'am

Let's consider practical issues related to communicating with parents. We'll start with the talking aspect of communication and then move on to the tougher listening part.

Here are the questions parents often ask about activities and events their kids are involved in. When the information you supply answers these questions, parents will know that you understand their needs and appreciate the responsibilities they have toward their teens.

INCOMPLETE INFORMATION:

Meet at the church Friday night, and we'll head out to go bowling.

COMPLETE INFORMATION:

Meet in the lower parking lot of the church at 6:45 p.m. on Friday, May 17th. The bus will be leaving at 7:00 sharp to go to the Redneck Bowlodrome at 1234 McKinley Street. We've got lanes booked from 7:15 to 9:00. We will be back at the church by 9:30 for pizza and awards. We'll wrap up by 10:15.

Make sure parents have the complete picture when it comes to cost. Camp might be $300, but what about...
— $6 for the lunch stop at Burgers and Burps on the way to camp
— $10 for parasailing
— $4 for the twice-daily trip to the Snack Shack
— $15 for the theme T-shirt
— $15 for the go-kart track where you traditionally stop at on the way home

- *Why?*
  — What is the purpose of the program or event?
  — What are you planning to accomplish?
  — What is the benefit of their child being involved?

- *Who?*
  — Who's invited? Junior high? Senior high? Both?
  — Should students invite friends?
  — Who's in charge?
  — Who's the point person?

- *When?*
  — What's the date?
  — When does it start?
  — When does it end?

- *Where?*
  — Where will you meet?
  — Where will you go from there?
  — Where will you end up?

- *Transportation?*
  — Who will be driving? (Few parents want their 16-year-old in a car driven by someone else's 16-year-old. Communicate that you have the safety of their kids in mind by having adults do the driving.)
  — What public transportation will you be taking?

- *Costs?*
  — What are the obvious costs?
  — What are the hidden costs?

  — $6 for the lunch stop at Burgers and Burps on the way to camp
  — $10 for parasailing
  — $4 for the twice-daily trip to the Snack Shack
  — $15 for the theme T-shirt
  — $15 for the go-kart track where you traditionally stop at on the way home

- *How to get in touch?*
  — What's the phone number of the camp, climbing-wall gym, or riding stables?
  — What's the number of your cell phone or pager?

Parent Point Web Site

Establish a Web site where parents can get information on upcoming events, see pictures from youth group events, and find links to Web sites of interest to parents. Find a parent (or student) who's skilled and interested and have them act as Webmaster for your site.

Bulletin Boards

Install a bulletin board for parents in a major traffic area of the church.

Most youth groups have bulletin boards for announcements, posters, pictures of events, and other youth group info, but often most parents don't see it because it's located in an out-of-the-way area near or in the youth room.

Post items on the board that will be of special interest to parents: reviews of current movies with suitability ratings, book reviews of new parenting resources (especially if they've been added to your church library), newspaper and magazine articles dealing with adolescent issues or parenting themes, pictures of youth group activities, details about upcoming events, and family-of-the-month (or week) profiles with pictures.

If you're going to put up a bulletin board, keep it up to date. Change something on the board every week, and give it a major overhaul once a month. This is a great project for a parent volunteer.

Parent Information Line

For groups with busy schedules, a dedicated phone line is a good investment. Use it with a voice-mail system to give parents details about upcoming events. The message should include the details: who the event is for, where it will be held, transportation arrangements, when and where parents can pick up their kids, costs, and any unusual details like costume themes ('70s bowling) or special clothing (bring jackets, hats, and gloves, because we'll be playing hide-and-seek in the freezer at the meat packing plant).

Remind parents of the cell phone or pager number they can use to contact you while the event is on. Just for fun, check with the phone company to see whether the last four digits of your phone number can be 4636 (info) in your exchange.

Missions Trip or Retreat Webcam

Give parents a first-hand look at what's happening on your retreat, service project, or missions trip by setting up a webcam to broadcast live images or streaming video to your youth group Web site. It will give them an opportunity to stay in touch with the group while you're away and also let them know that

For great youth group clip art, get *ArtSource CD-ROM Clip Art Library Version 3.0* or *ArtSource Youth Group Activities* (2003), published by Youth Specialties.

staying connected with you matters. For help with the webcam technology, go to webcamworld.com.

If the technology for a live feed isn't available, you can shoot short digital video clips or digital stills each day and post them on the Web site. Let the students share prayer requests, answers to prayer, and highlights of the day. Parents will love checking for their kids. Make sure each kid gets roughly the same amount of "playing time." It's disheartening for parents to search in vain for their kid, only to find more of the one who hogs the spotlight.

All the News That's Fit to Print

A regularly published parent newsletter provides an ideal forum for informing families about the details of your youth ministry program. In larger, more heavily programmed ministries, a monthly newsletter with a calendar insert is a good goal, while smaller ministries can be effective with a quarterly or seasonal issue. With computer programs that make publishing easy, you can create a parent information newsletter on a regular basis.

Even if you cut and paste the newsletter, a little clip art and some fun fonts can make it look good.

The tough part isn't the layout or production; it's making sure the newsletter contains accurate, up-to-date information of enough substance to be worth reading. Make sure your production has a quality, first-class look to it. If you put your effort into it, you want parents to read it, not trash it! Like it or not, the newsletter is one more aspect for parents to evaluate your professionalism.

Have a look at the sample newsletter included in the sidebar to give you a feel for the look you can create with relative ease.

Here are a few hints to help you produce a quality newsletter:

- Establish and maintain a consistent look for your publication so parents will recognize it. Include regular features (Q&A, All about Teen Development) parents can look forward to.

- Publish dates for upcoming events, giving plenty of advance notice. Check the **Windows of Warning** article (page 42) for guidelines. If you offer lots of activities, insert a monthly calendar with details.

- Make sure your ministry mission statement is visible in each issue. It will be a good reminder to parents of what the youth ministry is trying to accomplish. (Excuse me? Did you say you don't have one? Shame on you! Have a look at *Purpose-Driven Youth Ministry* by Doug Fields (Zondervan, 2000) for ideas about how to put one together.)

- Check to see if a local college student (journalism or graphic design major) is available to help with the newsletter. It might be a perfect class project for them, and—who knows?—it might turn into their piece of the youth ministry pie.

- Use digital photos to bring life to your layout. Make sure the exposure is good and details are visible on the newsletter copies. Sometimes the original pictures look great but copy terribly. Be careful not to feature the same kids over and over. In fact, look for opportunities to feature some of the less charismatic kids as a way to affirm them and encourage their parents.

- Don't use a lot of fonts on the same page. It makes the page look messy and unreadable. Pick one or two font families (regular, bold, italics, etc.) for the heads and one font for body text.

- Start a file folder in your bottom drawer to stash material for your next issue—cartoons, jokes statistical graphs from *USA Today*, event details, media reviews, quotes from *Youthworker* journal or books you're reading, local news of interest to parents, etc.

- Publish extra copies of your newsletter for parents to give out to other parents at work or in their neighborhoods. Remember that potential audience as you put together each issue.

- If you are create your newsletter electronically, post it on your church's Web site or link it to your youth ministry site.

- Check out the ready-made parent newsletter at www.theparentlink.com. You simply download the current issue, drop in your local details, and click print! It doesn't get much easier than that. Annual subscription.

Learning to Listen

Most of us are far better talkers than listeners. Even when we're listening, we can't wait for the other person to be done so we can take charge of the conversation again. Many youth workers find *listening* to parents difficult.

DIALOGUES OF THE DEAF

Listen to all the conversations of our world, those between nations as well as those between couples. They are for the most part dialogues of the deaf. Each one speaks primarily in order to set forth his own ideas, in order to justify himself, in order to enhance himself and to accuse others. Exceedingly few exchanges of viewpoints manifest a real desire to understand the other person.

Paul Tournier, *To Understand Each Other* (John Knox Press, 1974), page 8

In Chapter 7 we'll talk about establishing a Parent Council as a way of establishing a formal feedback process from select parents, but at this level, we're simply talking about listening to individual parents. What are some specific things we ought to be listening for?

Listen to parents' questions. When parents ask questions, it's usually because they need more information. You may think you've communicated information adequately, but if you still find parents asking questions, you may have forgotten information, not been clear, or made assumptions…or they may haven't read the flier. Use parent questions as cues for clarification.

Listen to parents' ideas. We often assume we have the corner on creativity. We've read the books, attended the seminars, and taken the classes. In many churches, youth workers are the designated idea person. In spite of it all, we'll do well to listen to the ideas that parents have for our youth ministries. They want the best for their kids, are familiar with the community, and probably have experience beyond ours. I've received some great ideas for games, special events, fundraisers, and teaching topics from parents over the years—and often with the idea comes with a willingness to help make the suggestion happen.

A word to the wise: when you listen to the ideas of parents be sure that your act of listening isn't interpreted as your enthusiastic endorsement. Some parents assume that, because you listen to their ideas, you are committing to act on them. Be gentle, but help them understand the difference

Listen to parents' side of the story. Two people can have different perspectives on the same events. This is especially true of adolescents and parents. I can't count the number of times I've created a portrait of a parent in my mind based on the information I've been fed by the disgruntled kid. Later, when I meet the parent from hell, I'm often amazed at how emotionally healthy and mentally balanced the parent is. When we take the time to listen to both sides of the story, we can get a clearer picture of reality.

Listen to parents' advice. Proverbs 19:20 says, "Listen to advice and accept instruction and in the end you will be wise."
You might be surprised to know that lots of parents are actually anxious to make you look good by supporting you in your ministry. If a caring parent gently shares a word of advice that seems to come out of nowhere, there's a good possibility they have heard a comment or sensed a problem you aren't

> The first to present his case seems right till another comes forward and questions him.
>
> Proverbs 18:17

aware of and are trying to save you from some grief you may not even realize is around the corner.

A humble, teachable spirit may be the most important qualification for a youth worker who wants to develop a parent ministry. If parents know you're listening, they can save you plenty of trouble. Of course know-it-alls who don't care about you at all also exist. But don't assume every advice-giving parent is out to get you.

Listen to parents' concerns. We are positioned to serve families and work alongside parents for the good of their kids and the health of their homes. If ministry emphasis or methods create legitimate concern, we are well advised to pay attention. Parents who express concern may be speaking on behalf of other parents who don't have the courage or the rapport to express those concerns. Some parents may not be gentle or gracious in their expressions of unease, but if we're gracious in receiving, we will probably benefit.

Listen to parents' gratitude. If we've taken the time to listen to the questions, perspectives, ideas, advice, and concerns of parents, we're likely to have the opportunity to listen to expressions of gratitude, too. A spirit of teamwork often develops into thankfulness, and many parents will find meaningful and practical ways to express it. Our motivation for ministry isn't to get thanks, but don't feel guilty about enjoying it when it comes.

With Pen in Hand

Sometimes you will find it helpful to gather demographics, interests, and concerns in writing from the entire lot at one time. On pages 47-50 you'll find **Family Needs Assessment**, a survey you can use or adapt. Spring might be a good time to distribute it, since that gives you the time to collect the completed assessments, tabulate and analyze the results, and adjust your autumn programming accordingly.

Delegate the process of compiling and sorting data to a qualified volunteer. Or hire a business or accounting instructor or student from a local community college. Appoint a commission to analyze and summarize the results. Give a report to church leadership, including recommendations. The leadership can then decide on specific courses of action and give a final report to the congregation along with specific changes that might be implemented.

• • •

Date: _____

Your candid responses enable our church to better meet the needs of your family members. Please answer as truthfully and accurately as you can. All information will be kept in the strictest confidence.

1. Please list all of the adults who are currently part of your household

_____

Name of adult completing this assessment: _____

❑ **Male**   ❑ **Female**   **Age:** _____   **Education level:** _____

Occupation (check one or two)
❑ Student
❑ Military
❑ Self-employed
❑ Homemaker
❑ Skilled trade (carpenter, electrician)
❑ Skilled worker (administrator, sales)
❑ Professional
❑ Management
❑ Retired
❑ Unemployed

Marital status
❑ Single, never married
❑ Single, divorced
❑ Single, widowed
❑ Separated
❑ Married to first spouse
❑ Widowed and remarried
❑ Divorced and remarried

If married, years married to present spouse
❑ 2 years or less
❑ 3-6 years
❑ 7-14 years
❑ 15-29 years
❑ 30 or more years

2. **If you are a parent, list children living at home.** (Use the back of this sheet if you need more room.)

Name _____ Age _____ Grade _____ ❑ Male ❑ Female
Name _____ Age _____ Grade _____ ❑ Male ❑ Female
Name _____ Age _____ Grade _____ ❑ Male ❑ Female
Name _____ Age _____ Grade _____ ❑ Male ❑ Female

3. **How long have you attended this church?**
❑ 2 years or less
❑ 3-5 years
❑ 6-10 years
❑ 11-19 years
❑ 20 or more years

4. **About how often do you attend church services and activities?**
❑ Less than once per month
❑ Once or twice per month
❑ Once per week
❑ Two or more times per week

5. **List family members and extended family who live in the area.** (Use the back of this sheet if you need more room.)
Name _____ Relationship _____
Name _____ Relationship _____
Name _____ Relationship _____
Name _____ Relationship _____

6. **If you are a parent, check the top five areas of concern regarding your children:**
❑ Communication
❑ School achievement
❑ Alcohol and drugs
❑ Sex and sexuality
❑ Discipline
❑ Expectations
❑ Father's role
❑ Mother's role
❑ Relationship with Christ
❑ Friendships and peer relations
❑ Media—television, video games, music
❑ The Internet
❑ Lack of social skills
❑ College and career
❑ Other _____

Family Needs Assessment

 (see page 46)

7. If you are presently married, check the top five areas of concern in your marriage

❑ Communication
❑ Time together
❑ Spirituality
❑ Trust
❑ Friendship
❑ Money
❑ Future
❑ Fulfillment
❑ Sex
❑ Substance abuse
❑ Pornography
❑ Physical or sexual abuse
❑ Conflict resolution
❑ Differences
❑ Career-home life balance
❑ Parents or in-laws
❑ Other ________________

8. What are the best times for members of your household to be involved in church-sponsored program?

(List members next to their best times.)

❑ Sunday mornings ________________
❑ Sunday afternoons________________
❑ Sunday evenings ________________
❑ Monday mornings ________________
❑ Monday afternoons ________________
❑ Monday evenings ________________
❑ Tuesday mornings ________________
❑ Tuesday afternoons ________________
❑ Tuesday evenings ________________
❑ Wednesday mornings ________________
❑ Wednesday afternoons ________________
❑ Wednesday evenings ________________
❑ Thursday mornings ________________
❑ Thursday afternoons ________________
❑ Thursday evenings ________________
❑ Friday mornings ________________
❑ Friday afternoons ________________
❑ Friday evenings ________________
❑ Saturday mornings ________________
❑ Saturday afternoons ________________
❑ Saturday evenings ________________

❑ Weekend retreats (one night) ________________
❑ Weekend retreats (two nights) ________________

If you need more room to answer any of the following four questions, use the back of this sheet.

9. What do you think is being done well at our church?

10. What do you think might be improved at our church? What suggestions do you have for improvements?

11. How can our church help you and your family?

12. How can our church help you become more connected to other church attenders?

Adapted from *The Youth Worker's Handbook to Family Ministry* by Chap Clark Copyright © 1997 by Youth Specialties.

Getting Together

A parent-teen workshop to improve family communication

The *Big* Idea

Getting Together is a family workshop designed to give teenagers and their parents a nonthreatening opportunity to communicate with one another in healthy new ways.

Beginning at the Beginning

The Target Group

This workshop is designed for families with teenagers who are in the seventh grade and up. Preteens are not likely to benefit from the activities and discussion topics. Help families who have teens and preteens understand that this event is specifically for parents and *teens*.

 The workshop format is based on at least one parent and one teenager from a family attending. Because of the intensely interactive nature of the material, kids coming without a parent or parents coming without at least one of their kids is nearly pointless. Make sure this is clear when you promote the event. If parentless kids or kidless parents show up, it will be tough to make the family times of discussion practical and personal.

Promoting the Event

This event isn't easy. Even though most families want improved communication, the idea of making it happen is scary—for kids and parents. Asking them to come to an event *together* makes this even more of a challenge. Unfortunately, many families aren't used to *being* together, much less *talking* to each other for an hour or two.

 "If you build it they will come," is a successful philosophy in *Field of Dreams*, but you can't assume it works for you and this event. Parents may be afraid that attending a workshop like this is an admission of failure or a public declaration of their family's dysfunction. Here are some ways you can make it easier for people.

- *Promote positively.* In advertising this event, make sure everyone knows that it's designed to make good family communication even better. Keep your promotional material upbeat and fun.

- *Make a party of it.* Consider including the workshop as part of a bigger event full of fun and food. Think about pizza, build your own banana split, a burger barbecue, or a Saturday morning (not too early) pancake breakfast. Tie it to an afternoon car rally or parents-versus-kids baseball game, and you'll have a better chance of getting people to come.

- *Move with the movers.* Include three or four mature, influential families in the planning and promotion process. Events with adults work the same way as they do with teenagers: if the cool people are coming, everyone comes. If not…

- *Offer them a taste.* Pick one of the games or discussion starters from the workshop (or use one of the other events in this book) to promote the workshop as an announcement in church or at another family event.

- *Feature the benefits rather than the need.* Instead of saying things like, "Does your family have a hard time spending more than a few minutes together in the same room?" or "Has it been too long since your family had a discussion without it turning into a big giant fight?" promote the event by saying, "You'll get a chance to talk together about the ways you deal with differing opinions," or "It'll be an evening of talking about the things that matter to everyone in your family."

- *Give them lots of warning.* Families are busy. Plan and promote well in advance.

Getting Set Up

> **You'll need...**
> - Moveable chairs
> - CD and CD player
> - Welcome table and a chair
> - Nametags
> - A volunteer host

Hold this workshop in a comfortable room, flexible and inviting. Use movable seating because you want to encourage lots of talking in family groups. (It's a communication workshop, remember?) So it won't work well with straight rows of chairs or church pews.

Start the evening with chairs set up in horseshoes of six to eight seats with the open end toward the front of the room. That way several family groups can sit together. This will help include single parents families and newly attending families.

Add to the ambience by playing upbeat music playing before people start to arrive. Favor the musical tastes of your teens, since parents are more likely to put up with kid-friendly music than kids will put up with adult favorites.

Set up a welcome table where people can get name tags. Don't assume everyone knows one another's name. Have a volunteer host giving directions at the table. Participants need to write first names only on their name tag. Last names create formality we don't need, and besides, with family structures being what they are these days, you can have multiple surnames in the same family. Provide a variety of colored markers and ask families to use the same color for all family members.

They're Here! They're Here!

An event like this needs to get off to a good start. Teens and parents may be apprehensive about what will happen when they "talk". Nothing will kill the mood more quickly than having parents and kids standing around awkwardly waiting for something to happen. Select one or both of the following activity options to get families working together as soon as they arrive.

When it's time to start the workshop, start—even though everyone hasn't had the same amount of time for the presession activity. The options take about five minutes to complete.

Tower Time

You'll need...
- 25 straws for each family
- A lump of modeling clay for each family (or 12 pieces of bubble gum for each person)
- Scissors, optional

Give each family group 25 drinking straws and a lump of modeling clay. (A fun option is to give everyone a dozen pieces of bubble gum to chew and use) Instruct them to work together as a family to design and construct the tallest freestanding tower they can with the supplies you've given them. If you want, make scissors available so they can cut the straws.

After admiring one another's feats of engineering, you can transition to the next activity by saying—

 **Working together to get a job done takes some communication, doesn't it? What would be the result if you all hadn't been able to talk to each other as you were working?**

You might hear answers like these: one person might take over, people end up feeling left out, we can't benefit from the creativity of others as much, there's no shared sense of accomplishment when the job is done.

Family Coat of Arms

You'll need...
- Markers
- Copies of **Family Coat of Arms** (page 57)
- Large pieces of newsprint, optional
- Pins or tape, optional

Give each family group markers and a copy of **Family Coat of Arms** (page 57). If you'd like, give them large pieces of newsprint to reproduce the coat of arms on. With large paper, everyone in the family can contribute at the same time. Let them know a coat of arms represents important information about a family, so they should choose symbols to indicate information about their family: faith, heritage, interests, hobbies, et cetera, (and the family name somewhere on the paper).

The artwork can be displayed on the walls of the meeting room when completed.

Ask parents and kids to share briefly about family discoveries while working on the project.

We're the Best! We're the Worst!

You'll need...
- Copies of **We're the Best! We're the Worst!** (page 58), one per person
- Transparency of **We're the Best! We're the Worst!** (page 58), optional
- Overhead projector, optional

By now it should be time to start, so ask people to move to the clusters of chairs you've set up with at least two different family groups in each.

Hand out copies of **We're the Best! We're the Worst!** (page 58) or make it into an transparency and project it. Have families pick two or three of the options to tell. Don't let this drag. Some families are more talkative than others, so pay attention and stop the conversations before they get tedious.

Good News, Bad News

Ask the kids to move to one side of the room and divide into groups of three to five, and have the parents do the same on the other side of the room. Have siblings and spouses split up as much as possible to get families spread out. Give each teen a copy of **P-A-R-E-N-T-S** (page 59), and give each parent a copy of **O-U-R-K-I-D-S** (page 60). Have them work together in their age-specific groups to generate lists of adjectives to describe the good and bad they see in the other generation.

Help them be lighthearted about the activity, not heavy or accusing. It's really just a chance for kids to be with other kids and parents to be with other parents to get the conversations going.

After they've had enough time to get at least one positive and one negative word for each of the letters have them regroup as individual family units. Encourage them to position their chairs so that they're sitting knee to knee in individual family circles. This will enable them to talk with each other easily.

Get general responses about whether people thought it was easier to think of positive words or negative words and why that might be so.

Have parents read their negative lists to the kids and then pick one word that they would use to describe themselves. Have kids to the same with their negative words. Don't let people slow down here or get too analytical. Move quickly to the positive lists, only this time, after parents read the lists have them identify one positive quality from the list that they see in each child. Repeat the process with kids affirming parent qualities.

Would We Rather...?

Point out that they've all started communicating, but that you want to help them keep up the process. Family units should stay together for this activity. Distribute **Would We Rather...?** (page 61, one per family.

The purpose of this discussion starter is to see how many of the 12 statements they can find family agreement on. Set the tone for *fun!* and debrief by finding out which family has the most disagreement and which family has the least. How many families were able to fully agree on half the statements or more?

Debrief by saying something like "Obviously even families who get along pretty well can't agree on everything, but we can always learn to be more effective in the ways we communicate with each other."

What Is Communication?

Move people back into their original multifamily clusters. Hand out copies of **What Is Communication?** (page 62) and pens. The handout begins by asking for comparisons of communication to games they're familiar with.

Give them a couple of examples to get the creativity flowing:

- Communication is like bowling when people fire their thoughts down the alley, aiming them toward the target. It takes lots of practice to keep ideas out of the gutter.

- In tennis the ball goes back and forth. In communication, ideas are tossed back and forth, take turns serving and responding

After they've taken a few minutes on this, ask for opinions on which game they think best symbolizes good communication. Then focus their attention on the definition near the bottom of the page. Have them decide whether they like the definition as it is or whether they would like to write their own definition of communication. Give them a few minutes to work as multiple family groups on the definition and then debrief.

Hopefully they will have discovered flaws in the printed definition. It's not a bad definition for one person's role in the process, but the definition doesn't address how communication involves listening. Let people share their revisions. Affirm their thoughts, but be sure everyone understands the reciprocal nature of communication.

Wrap up this section by talking about the fact that most people find listening to be the hardest part of good communication.

Listen Up! Reverse Charades

You'll need...
- A transparency of **Emotional Emotions** (page 63)
- Overhead projector
- A stopwatch

Explain that one of the toughest parts of listening is to pick up on the emotions that often lie beneath the words spoken. The words themselves tell only part of the story.

This unusual version of a familiar game will help your group tune in to emotions we communicate. This is reverse charades: the acting is done by the crowd and the guessing is done by the individuals upfront. Invite four adults and four teens to be the guessers in the front of the room; have them face the crowd with their backs to the screen—parents on one side of you, teens on the other. Keep track of each team's total time with the stopwatch.

Have one parent guesser step forward (each individual guesses alone) and all the audience parent stand. The audience parents act out the emotion you reveal on the overhead while their guesser guesses. Reveal *impatient* and start the stopwatch! When the parents guess, the kids get up and repeat the process with *frustrated*. Remember, unlike traditional charades, in this version the crowd acts and the person upfront guesses.)

For a little extra fun or to break a tie, show the final word *constipated*. Have the whole crowd stand up and let all eight guessers guess. It might be a good time to have a video camera panning the crowd!

Communication Killers

You'll need...
- Copies of **Communication Killers** (page 64), one for each person
- Pens, one for each person

Move people back into their knee-to-knee individual family formation, distribute **Communication Killers** (page 64) and say something along these lines—

> **Most of us would agree that *not listening* is the biggest communication killer, but people develop plenty of other bad habits when it comes to family communication. Some bad habits have plagued families forever.**

Give everyone a few minutes to work individually and to jot initials of family members beside whichever bad communication patterns apply to each. Then star one or two bad habits that they think apply to themselves.

Now, with a parent going first, they should look over the list to guess which ones family members picked for the parent. Let other family members guess in whatever order they'd like.

Wrap up the exercise by encouraging each family member to pick one bad habit to work on improving during the next week. They can ask family members for gentle reminders when they fall into old patterns. Remind everyone that it's important to claim our bad habits and ask for help with them.

The Word on Good Communication

> **You'll need...**
> - Copies of **The Word on Our Words** (page 65-66), one for each family
> - Pens, one for each person

Say:

> **Most of our discussion so far has been about problems we have in communication, not listening very well and other bad habits we've gotten into. Let's wrap up our workshop on a positive note.**

Give each family **The Word on Our Words** (page 65-66). Have them carefully review the four passages of scripture and work together on the responses. The verses are practical instructions for positive communication.

Allow parents to exercise leadership as they discuss the principles. Give them 10 to 20 minutes for discussion and filling in the accountability form at the end.

Close in prayer, committing parents and teenagers to the Lord. Encourage them to follow through with what they've learned.

Serve snacks to wrap up the evening.

Family Coat of Arms

(see page 53)

Work together as a family to fill each space on your coat of arms.

Key

1. Stick-figure pictures of everyone in our family with some clue that identifies who each person is (golf club, book, hair style).

2. A picture of what we do to play—family fun we all enjoy together (miniature golf, Monopoly).

3. A picture of where we live (neighborhood, city, house).

4. A picture of our family's favorite fast food or our favorite at home-cooked meal.

5. A symbol of a family tradition (something we love to do over and over again).

6. A creative version of our family's last-name initial.

What's the best family
vacation we've ever had?

What's the worst pet
our family has ever had?

What's the best
practical joke someone
in our family has
ever pulled off?

What's the worst weather we
ever experienced together?

WHAT'S THE BEST THING THAT'S HAPPENED
TO OUR FAMILY IN THE PAST YEAR?

 ## WHAT'S THE WORST
meal we ever had?

What's the best gift our family has ever received?

What's the worst car
we ever owned?

WHAT'S THE BEST PLACE OUR
FAMILY HAS EVER LIVED?

What's the worst experience we ever had with a neighbor?

what's the best quality of
one member of our family?

P-A-R-E-N-T-S

(see page 54)

Think of **positive** words beginning with the letters below that describe parents who are working hard to make their families a good place to belong.

P
A
R
E
N
T
S

Think of **negative** words beginning with the letters below that describe parents who aren't working hard at making their families a good place to belong.

P
A
R
E
N
T
S

O-U-R-K-I-D-S

(see page 54)

Think of **positive** words beginning with the letters below that describe kids who are working hard to make their families a good place to belong.

O
U
R
K
I
D
S

Think of **negative** words beginning with the letters below that describe kids who aren't working hard at making their families a good place to belong.

O
U
R
K
I
D
S

Would We Rather...?
(see page 54)

Would we rather...

...vacation in the summer at the beach or in the winter in the mountains?

...HAVE CHINESE OR PIZZA DELIVERED WHEN NOBODY FEELS LIKE COOKING?

...play a game or watch a movie?

...EAT OUT AT FAST FOOD PLACES A LOT OR GO OUT FOR A NICE FAMILY DINNER LESS OFTEN?

...go camping or stay in hotels?

...RIDE ROLLER COASTERS OR VISIT MUSEUMS?

...spend Christmas Day with relatives or alone as a family?

...HAVE HAM OR TURKEY AT THANKSGIVING?

...have a cat or a dog as a family pet?

...GET A JET-SKI OR A SNOWMOBILE?

...listen to an oldies station or talk radio when traveling?

...SIT TOGETHER IN CHURCH OR SCATTER AND SIT WITH FRIENDS?

From *Youth Worker's Guide to Parent Ministry* by Marv Penner. Permission to reproduce this page granted only for use in the buyer's own youth group. Copyright © 2003 by Youth Specialties. www.YouthSpecialties.com/store/downloads Password: pride

What Is Communication?

(see page 54)

How is communication **LiKE BoWLiNG?**

LiKE TENNiS?

LiKE BASEBALL?

LiKE CHESS?

LiKE HoCKEY?

LiKE FooTBALL?

LiKE CHARADES?

Defining Communication

Think about this definition of communication:

Communication: is the process of sharing yourself verbally and nonverbally so that another person can both accept and understand what you are sharing with him or her.

How would you edit the definition to make it more accurate? Rewrite a definition of communication that your group can agree on.

impatient

frustrated

BITTER

fearful

anxious

ECSTATIC

EXHAUSTED

Arrogant

Bonus:

(constipated)

Communication Killers

(see page 55)

Jot initials of family members beside bad communication patterns that apply to them. Place a star by one or two bad habits that apply to you.

No eye contact
How would you know I'm connecting with you?

_____   _____   _____

Big or abstract words
What do you mean you don't know what I mean?

_____   _____   _____

Speaking for the other person
I know what you would have said.

_____   _____   _____

Clichés and pat answers
No problem! It's all good!

_____   _____   _____

Yelling
Maybe if I say it louder you'll get it.

_____   _____   _____

Gossip and slander
Talking about people behind their backs.

_____   _____   _____

Nagging
I know you know, but I need to tell you again anyway.

_____   _____   _____

Putting people down
Was that your character I just assassinated?

_____   _____   _____

Critical attitude
I think I can find some fault here somewhere.

_____   _____   _____

Rationalizing, justifying, and defending
I have a good excuse for everything.

_____   _____   _____

Pretending not to hear
I can be deaf when I need to be.

_____   _____   _____

The silent treatment
I'll talk when I feel like it...which isn't now.

_____   _____   _____

Overly emotional
This could win me an Academy Award.

_____   _____   _____

Sarcasm and cheap shots
Let me bring you down a notch or two.

_____   _____   _____

Changing the subject
Let's talk about what I want to talk about.

_____   _____   _____

TV, newspaper, or computer absorption
Just can't tear myself away.

_____   _____   _____

Here's some practical advice from the Bible to make your family better for everyone. Read each biblical principle together and discuss the questions.

BEING ONE IN SPIRIT AND PURPOSE, DO NOTHING OUT OF SELFISH AMBITION OR VAIN CONCEIT, BUT IN HUMILITY CONSIDER OTHERS BETTER THAN YOURSELVES. EACH OF YOU SHOULD LOOK NOT ONLY TO YOUR OWN INTERESTS, BUT ALSO TO THE INTERESTS OF OTHERS.

—PHILIPPIANS 2:2-4

- WHO'S THE LEAST SELFISH PERSON IN YOUR FAMILY?

- WHAT'S A FAMILY GOAL OR PURPOSE THAT EVERYONE SHARES AND CONTRIBUTES TO?

- WHAT'S AN IMMEDIATE CHANGE YOU'D NOTICE IN YOUR HOME IF YOU ALL LIVED BY THIS PRINCIPLE? (THINK: THE TV REMOTE, THE CAR, THE FRIDGE, THE BATHROOM, CHORES, ETC.)

DO NOT LET ANY UNWHOLESOME TALK COME OUT OF YOUR MOUTHS BUT ONLY WHAT IS HELPFUL FOR BUILDING ONE ANOTHER UP ACCORDING TO THEIR NEEDS THAT IT MAY BENEFIT THOSE WHO LISTEN.

—EPHESIANS 4:29

- WHAT ARE THREE OR FOUR KINDS OF UNWHOLESOME TALK IN YOUR FAMILY?

- WHAT HAS SOMEONE IN YOUR FAMILY SAID RECENTLY THAT HAS BUILT YOU UP?

- WHAT'S AN AREA THAT YOU COULD USE ENCOURAGEMENT IN RIGHT NOW?

CLOTHE YOURSELVES WITH COMPASSION, KINDNESS, HUMILITY, GENTLENESS AND PATIENCE. BEAR WITH ONE ANOTHER AND FORGIVE WHATEVER GRIEVANCES YOU MAY HAVE AGAINST ONE ANOTHER. FORGIVE AS THE LORD FORGAVE YOU.

—COLOSSIANS 3:12-13

- IF BEARING WITH ONE ANOTHER IS LIKE PATIENTLY PUTTING UP WITH SOMEONE, WHAT'S AN AREA FOR YOU TO BEAR TODAY OR THIS WEEK?

- WHAT'S YOUR FAMILY PATTERN OF HANDLING APOLOGIES AND FORGIVENESS?

- HOW IS YOUR FORGIVENESS PATTERN THE SAME AND HOW IS IT DIFFERENT FROM HOW THE LORD FORGAVE YOU?

FINALLY ALL OF YOU, LIVE IN HARMONY WITH ONE ANOTHER

—1 PETER 3:8

- WHAT ARE SOME REASONS THAT HARMONY, A MUSICAL WORD, IS A GOOD PICTURE OF A FAMILY THAT'S WORKING THE WAY IT SHOULD?

- FILL IN THE FORM BELOW. POST IT ON THE FRIDGE. DO YOUR PART FOR HARMONY!

MY WORD TO MY FAMILY

I UNDERSTAND THAT FAMILY COMMUNICATION DOESN'T HAPPEN WITHOUT EFFORT. WE ALL NEED TO DO OUR PART TO MAKE IT WORK. HERE'S SOMETHING I'M WILLING TO WORK ON IN THE NEXT TWO WEEKS:

ENCOURAGE ME WHEN YOU SEE IMPROVEMENT AND LET ME KNOW WHEN I'M MESSING UP.

_____   _____
SIGNED   DATE

Chapter 4

Have You Hugged a Parent Today?

Encourage Parents in their Role and Responsibilities

"Encouragment gives hope."

"All the leadership and people-managment training and experience in the world seem irrelevant when it comes to kids."

"A word aptly spoken is like apples of gold in settings of silver."

Parenting is a long journey. Sometimes the road is flat and smooth; more often it's rocky and uphill. The destination is difficult to keep in view, so travelers don't always know if they're making progress. Many feel overwhelmed, frustrated, or even hopeless.

As youth workers, we're uniquely positioned to encourage moms and dad on the parenting journey. When parents experience fear, face exhaustion, or lack resolve in difficult circumstances, encouragement gives them hope.

We have the basis for encouragement: we know their kids. We see them week after week, Sunday after Sunday, in a variety of settings. In many cases we've watched them grow from early adolescence into young adulthood.

We have opportunities for encouragement (whether naturally or intentionally occurring). We encounter parents during all-church activities; at sporting events, community events, or concerts; and as they drop off and pick up their kids.

We have the means to communicate encouragement: we pass in the church hallway, visit their homes, chat on the phone, send e-mails and letters.

All we need to remember is to *do* it!

Why Parents Need Encouragement

Parenting adolescents can be a lonely, thankless job.

Kids are developmentally programmed to pull away from mom and dad beginning during the early teen years. It's good, it's appropriate, it's right…and it's scary. Kids can be cruel as they seek their independence. "Drop me off a block from school, so nobody sees us together."

Get to know a few parents and you'll find that they feel the least competent when their kids are adolescents. I've seen many a CEO or successful professional crumble during the challenge of raising teenagers. All the leadership and people-management training and experience in the world seem irrelevant when it comes to their own kids.

Some people are dragging excess baggage.

When people become parents, almost all of them make promises to right the wrongs inflicted on them by their parents. "I'll do it right," they insist, perhaps unaware of the hurt or anger influencing their decisions.

When relationships begin to feel strained—as they are prone to every hour or two with teenagers—they often find themselves reverting back to unhealthy controlling or emotionally distancing patterns that can be destructive to relationships. They may abuse power, lose control of their anger, manipulate through emotions, slip into workaholism or other destructive addictions, detach emotionally, or appease others at any cost. Of course, when these strategies don't work and kids pull away even more, parents experience guilt, shame, and failure.

This is the stage of adulthood when parents are forced to deal with the end of life for their parents and the end of childhood for their children. It has potential to be an emotionally confusing and relationally unsettling time. A little encouragement goes a long way!

Parents may feel alone in their failures.

Parents are painfully aware of their blunders. They have an innate sense of how they're doing, even if their kids aren't reminding them of their mistakes. And when they compare themselves to other parents, they *know* they don't measure up. Unfortunately, in some churches it's difficult to be honest about what's *really* going on in our families. We strut only our successes and victories, remaining silent about difficult experiences and using masks to hide our true feelings.

It may seem unnecessary to encourage the mom or dad

- Why are some parents reluctant to admit struggles in their family?

- Church families are sometimes especially susceptible to dishonest posturing. Why do you suppose that is?

NAME NAMES

Write the names of one or two kids in your ministry by each adjective. Look for opportunities to let parents know about the qualities you see in their children.

caring **Joey**

genuine **Sarah**

energetic **Ken & Beth**

who appears successful at parenting. Until a family collapses into a crisis, we assume that everything is okay. In reality nearly all parents of teenagers live with some level of anxiety related to their role as parents. We can accurately assume that every parent in our circle of ministry will benefit from encouragement, whether they look like they need it or not.

As youth workers we're used to honesty. (Teenagers can be brutally honest!) So we're in a unique position to establish a climate of transparency in which parents can be equally honest and receive our encouragement without feeling guilty or exposed.

The Vocabulary of Encouragement

Parents love to hear about the positive characteristics of their sons and daughters. Start with the following list. Use it to get started in your ministry of encouraging parents. As you think of others, write them down.

ambitious	insightful
articulate	inquisitive
committed	kind
compassionate	loving
confident	mature
cooperative	optimistic
creative	patient
disciplined	pleasant
faithful	polite
friendly	reliable
fun	responsible
generous	sincere
gifted in… (name a specific area)	spiritually mature
gracious	thoughtful
happy	trustworthy
hardworking	unselfish
helpful	wise
honest	

_____   _____

_____   _____

_____   _____

_____   _____

Ideas for Encouragers

Encouragement can take many forms. Think about ways that people have encouraged you in the past. Use some of those methods to encourage parents. Then try these ideas:

A Word Aptly Spoken

The Bible reminds us in Proverbs 25:11 of the power of a well-timed word. It says, "A word aptly spoken is like apples of gold in settings of silver." In his letter to the church at Ephesus, Paul reminds his friends to use their words to encourage one another. He writes, "Do not let any unwholesome talk come out of your mouths, but only what is helpful for building others up according to their needs, that it may benefit those who listen." (Eph 4:29)

Over the course of any week of ministry, our paths will often cross briefly with parents. We bump into them in the church foyer, we sit with them on a board or committee, we see them dropping their kids off for an event, we meet them at a game or in the mall, or we find ourselves in their homes for one reason or another. Each of these encounters, no matter how quick or serendipitous, can create an opportunity for speaking a word of encouragement. **It doesn't take long for encouragement to become a habit, and it's a great way to discipline ourselves to think positively about each student in our care.** We all realize that adolescents are people in process and that we have plenty of opportunities to judge if we want to, but you rarely find a kid about whom you can't find something positive to say.

- *Affirm character qualities.* Often all parents notice is performance or achievement. Dad may be quick to see his daughter's win on the playing field or his son's accomplishment on stage but slow to see the character trait that lies beneath the success. They may need to have encouragement of character qualities modeled for them.

- *Affirm direction.* Even kids who are struggling will often show incremental improvement in significant area of their life. Parents may need to be reminded that direction is more important (and more attainable) than arrival at a destination.

- *Affirm effort.* Although there may be no visible evidence of success, you know that a kid has given a goal her best shot. Let parents know that you saw and appreciated the effort. Take care not to be condescending or patronizing.

REFLECT

Paul says our encouraging words should be rooted in an understanding of the needs of those we talk to. What are some of the specific needs of individual parents in your ministry? Which parent needs comfort? Wisdom? Patience? Financial help? Forgiveness? Support?

- *Affirm relationships.* Students' relationships touch the area of greatest fear for most parents. They realize the critical importance of the friends their teenager chooses. As youth workers we often see kids making good relational choices: handling a conflict well, standing up to peer pressure, ditching friends who are damaging, welcoming a new student into their friendship cluster, acting appropriately with a boyfriend or girlfriend on the bus trip, etc. Parents will always be thrilled to hear this kind of news.

Notes of Encouragement

Often parents are so surprised to hear us speak positively about their teenager that they miss the joy of hearing it. Spoken words hang in the air for the moment; then all that's left is the memory—nice but not concrete.

Written notes are tangible encouragements parents can savor. If your encouragement seems too good to be true the first time parents read it, they can read your note over and over again. They can put it under a pillow so that, at 2:00 a.m. when their teen still hasn't arrived home, they can refer back to it for some perspective. It's something they can show the kid's grandparents to give the older generation hope. A note of encouragement is a gift that keeps on giving.

Photocopy the postcards on pages 79-82 onto card stock. Keep a supply of them handy, so you can write some words of encouragement to a parent—who probably needs it more than you realize.

Free Postage

The next time your church or organization does a mailing, grab a half dozen of the letters going to parents of your students. Scrawl a quick note on the letter on the back of the envelope is sealed to make a parent's day: "I saw this letter heading to your house and thought I'd let you know that I loved having Sean on the canoe trip with us last month. What a good son you're raising. Give him a high five for me and ask him to tell you the beaver dam story."

I-Know-It's-Not-_Your_-Birthday Card

Send a short note of encouragement to the parents on the occasion of their child's birthday. It's one of those out-of-nowhere hugs that can mean a great deal to a parent. When kids have birthdays, parents are usually doing the giving. This is a chance for you to give to them: affirm the work they've done with their kid throughout the year.

Do-It-Yourself Postcards

At your next retreat, fundraiser, or service project, make sure that you get a picture of individual students in your group. Get double prints made, post one set of the pictures on your bulletin board as you normally would and use the other set as personalized postcards. Just write your encouraging note on the back, slap on the postage and drop it in the mail slot. Parents love seeing their kids having a good time.

Pass-It-On Encouragement

Call a parent who has an administrative assistant screening calls at work and, instead of asking for the parent, simply ask the assistant to pass along a message: "Tell her Monica called from the church. I just want her to know that I love having her son on our leadership team and that I've seen him take leadership with the sound system in the last few weeks. He's doing a great job." That kind of message will go a long way to give encouragement to a stressed parent during a hectic day of appointments and deadlines.

Beat-the-Kid-Home Encouragement

This is an encouragement idea I learned by accident one day, but I've used it many times since then to give parents—and kids—a bit of a boost.

We had just finished our Bible study, and I had popped into my office to grab an item while the kids were still hanging out. I had been impressed that evening with one student—Michelle. She had shown unusual maturity in the way she had processed the material and had spontaneously given leadership to a component of the study.

Because Michelle was normally somewhat shy, I knew that her parents would be excited to hear about her evening. Without much thought I grabbed the phone and made a two-minute call to her house. I told Michelle's parents that their daughter would have made them proud that evening, that they must be doing something right, and that I was honored to have their child in my youth group.

I didn't give the call another thought until about an hour later when my phone rang at home. It was Michelle. "What did you say to my parents?" she wanted to know. "I walked in the door, and they were waiting for me. They hugged me and told me how happy they were to be my parents, how proud of me they were."

A simple two-minute call and everybody wins. Since experiencing the impact of that brief conversation, I've often taken the time to beat the kid home with a word of encouragement. Parents always appreciate it.

When Encouragement Isn't Easy: Encouraging Parents Who Are Hurting

It's fun to encounter the parents whose kids are doing well. It's fairly easy to think of kind and affirming words, and making a call or jotting a quick note feels natural. Encouragement is much tougher with parents whose kids are legitimately struggling...

- The mom whose son just got arrested for shoplifting—again.
- The parents of the 16-year-old who just announced that she's having a baby.
- The dad of the sullen, angry 14-year-old who refuses to come to church and who's hanging out with the wrong people.
- The parents of the kid who disrupts every youth group event and causes you to think thoughts you later have to confess as sin.
- The parents of the 15-year-old who ran away from home three weeks ago and hasn't been heard from yet.
- The parents of the girl who committed suicide last year. They feel responsible somehow, and the guilt has been impossible to shake.

Happy families are all alike. Every unhappy family is unhappy in its own way.

Leo Tolstoy, *Anna Karenina*

These parents need our encouragement the most. How do you offer appropriate support to these hurting folks—especially when they are sometimes part of the problem?

This topic is addressed in more detail in the last chapter, Parent Ministry in Special Circumstances, but here are a few thoughts on encouraging these hurting parents of prodigals.

- Somehow try to get your heart around the immensity of the pain. The devastation is immense when parents have failed—or imagine they have failed. The pain doesn't go away. Some hurting parents report that the pain is worse than a death, because each day their hope is dashed anew.

- Don't belittle or trivialize the pain of a hurting parent. Comments like, "He's going through a phase," or "I was a rotten kid, too. It all works out in the end," are more damaging than helpful. Beware of carelessly quoting Bible verses. The only people who qualify to quote verses are those who have genuinely borne part of the burden. If you are able to participate with them in their pain, then perhaps they will be able to hear the comfort of Scripture you might share.

- When you've established a relationship of trust and parents have opened the door to the topic of their prodigal, you can appropriately pursue further conversation. Ask God to give you a heart of sincerity as you ask sensitive questions.

  — When was the last time you heard from Mark?
  — What's been the toughest part for your family as you've seen Jessie turn away from her faith?
  — What do you fear as you think about the future?

There's a fine line between concern and intrusion. Ask for wisdom in finding that line. And, **once you've entered into this level of dialogue with parents, don't suddenly abandon them. They've had plenty of rejection already.**

- Volunteer to support parents in prayer. Most of these parents are not naïve; they know they need a miracle. Ask them how you can specifically pray for their teen and—equally important—how you can pray for them as parents. If there are several families in this situation and if the parents are open to the idea, develop an intercessory prayer team who will faithfully pray for the family.

• • •

Aren't They Awesome!

A parent meeting to celebrate the good we see in our kids

A recurring complaint kids often make is that parents see only their failures. The problem—at least in part—is that many parents view themselves primarily as disciplinarians. Under the stress and pressure of keeping teenagers in line, they forget to focus on their good qualities.

The *Big* Picture

This session helps parents see positive traits in their teens and reveals practical ways to affirm their kids.

Affirmation Graffiti

You'll need...
- Butcher paper or newsprint
- Markers
- Tape or pins

Before parents arrive, create a large graffiti wall by covering an area with butcher paper or newsprint. Title the wall, OUR KIDS ARE AWESOME, and write the following words on the wall like graffiti: LOYAL FRIEND, HARDWORKING, SPIRITUALLY DISCIPLINED, CREATIVE, PROBLEM SOLVER, HUMBLE.

As parents come in, tell them that you've started the wall by writing down some qualities you've seen in their children. Give them a few markers and ask them to jot down a positive adjective or two describing *each of their teenagers* while others are still coming.

A Quick Look Back

Once you have a fairly comprehensive display of positive words (and everyone has added words to the wall) have parents sit down. They'll use the graffiti wall again later in the meeting.

Welcome everyone and explain that the agenda for the evening is to celebrate the good we see in our teenagers. Move them quickly into groups of three or four people, encouraging them to separate from their spouses.

Ask the groups to take some time to remember what it was like to be 14 again. Have them add 14 to their birth year to identify the year. Give them a moment to do the time warp needed to get into that early teenager frame of mind.

Have parents share an adjective their eighth or ninth grade teacher might have used to describe them. After everyone has had a turn, have them share an adjective that their parents would have used to describe them at 14. In the third round, share an adjective or two their friends would have used if they were asked.

Finally, and perhaps most importantly, have the group members think about an adjective that *only they* or their very closest friends would have known to be true. Say something like this—

> For most teenagers processes are happening inside that nobody else knows about. What one or two words would have been true of you, but which might have surprised your teachers, your parents, and perhaps even your friends?

Debrief by reminding parents that their kids live with the same mix of positive and negative perceptions. Parents have the opportunity—and responsibility—to speak encouragement into the lives of their teenagers.

Seeing the Potential in Our Kids

You'll need...
- Copies of **He Is...** (page 83), one for each person

Continue with an explanation along these lines—

> As parents you're in a position to see both the good and the bad in your kids. Have a look at this description of a kid and tell me if you'd be proud to have him as a son.

Pass out copies of He Is... Apologize for the lack of punctuation—some kind of computer glitch apparently—but assure them they'll have no trouble figuring it out. Most people will read the description ending the first sentence with the word wickedness and read through the entire piece with a negative spin.

If you identify a parent who is reading the paragraph negatively, have him read the description out loud. When finished, say something such as—

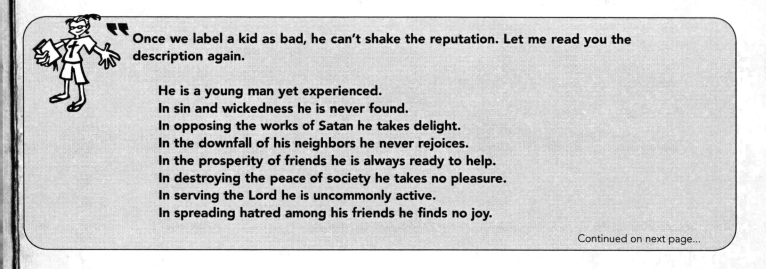

> Once we label a kid as bad, he can't shake the reputation. Let me read you the description again.
>
> He is a young man yet experienced.
> In sin and wickedness he is never found.
> In opposing the works of Satan he takes delight.
> In the downfall of his neighbors he never rejoices.
> In the prosperity of friends he is always ready to help.
> In destroying the peace of society he takes no pleasure.
> In serving the Lord he is uncommonly active.
> In spreading hatred among his friends he finds no joy.

Continued on next page...

... Continued

**In helping to promote the cause of Christianity he has been very active.
In attempting to tear down the church he makes no effort.
In trying to overcome his evil passions he works hard
To build up Satan's kingdom he lends no aid.
In spreading the gospel among heathen people he contributes daily.
To the devil he will never go.
To heaven he must go where he will receive his reward.**

Same kid. Different point of view. Let's ask God to see our own kids from his perspective. 🙶

God Sees Good Things in Kids

You'll need...
• A Bible

Apparently God sees the potential in young people; he often used young people to accomplish his purposes in the Scripture. As a whole group, brainstorm a list of young people in the Bible whom God used in significant ways.

They should come up with names like Joseph, Jeremiah, Daniel and his three friends, King Josiah, David, Mary the mother of Jesus, Timothy, and the kid who shared his lunch.

(Interestingly, many religious revivals have begun when young people have taken their faith seriously and chosen to live radically in response.)

First Timothy is a letter written by Paul, a loving mentor, to a young pastor, Timothy. Although Timothy probably wasn't an actual teenager, the spirit of the passage applies well to this discussion with parents. Have someone read 1 Timothy 4:12: "Don't let anyone look down on you because you are young, but set an example for the believers in speech, in life, in love, in faith and in purity."

Lead a brief discussion using the following questions to guide you:

• What are some reasons adults look down on young people?
• What are some ways that teenagers respond to being looked down on?
• In what ways does the church reinforce negative views of teenagers?

Ask people to get into groups so that at least three families are represented. Have them share responses to this question: Describe a specific incident when your child has been an example to you in speech, behavior, love, faith, or purity?"

Bring the entire group back together to hear outstanding examples. Ask for examples of how parents affirm their teenagers when they see them doing well. Parents can mentally file away ideas to use with their kids.

Back to the Graffiti Wall

You'll need...
- The graffiti wall used in the opening activity
- Lots of markers, plenty of colors

Ask parents to come back to the wall with a different colored marker for each of their children. Instruct them to underline all the qualities scattered on the wall that could describe their oldest teenager. Have them repeat the exercise for each of their children, underlining words in a color specific to that child. It'll be crowded as parents jockey for position and underline words. That's the whole idea!

Be sensitive to parents for whom the activity is difficult because their kids are struggling. Help them think of positive traits to affirm in their kids in spite of the fact that negative traits seem more obvious.

An Affirmation Exercise

You'll need...
- Transparency of **Aren't They Awesome?!** (page 84)
- Overhead projector
- Copies of the stationery (page 85)

Wrap up the meeting by giving parents an opportunity to affirm their teenagers by writing them letters. Give a few pointers by projecting the tips on **Aren't They Awesome?!** (page 84).

Review the list of characteristics we can affirm, noting that we often overlook these areas. Ask for other suggestions. Review the affirmation principles so they're fresh in their minds as they write letters to their kids. Pass out stationery (on page 85) and pens. Let parents take as many sheets as they have kids.

Encourage parents to write their letters before they go (or within the next 48 hours, if time is short). Suggest they find a creative way to get it into their kids' hands: slip it into a backpack, under a pillow, in their lunch, inside the bathroom medicine cabinet, on their car seat.

Close in prayer.

Don't set yourself up as a parenting expert if you're a young youth worker. Act as a facilitator projects humility.

Draw your own postcard here.

He is a young man yet experienced in sin and wickedness he is never found in opposing the works of Satan he takes delight in the downfall of his neighbors he never rejoices in the prosperity of friends he is always ready to help in destroying the peace of society he takes no pleasure in serving the Lord he is uncommonly active in spreading hatred among his friends he finds no joy in helping to promote the cause of Christianity he has been very active in attempting to tear down the church he makes no effort in trying to overcome his evil passions he works hard to build up Satan's kingdom he lends no aid in spreading the gospel among heathen people he contributes daily to the devil he will never go to heaven he must go where he will receive his reward

Affirm Our Teenagers

- Good-friend qualities

- Wise time management

- Financial discipline

- Spiritual passion

- Attitudes about circumstances they can't change

- Hopes and dreams for the future

- Sense of humor and fun

- Choice of friends

- Willingness to try new activities

- Promptness and punctuality

- Helping around the house and in the yard

- Appropriate fashion decisions

Affirmation Principles

- Affirm character qualities.

- Affirm progress. Don't wait for perfection.

- Don't qualify your affirmations. No "buts."

- Make affirmation a conscious habit.

- Affirm as soon as possible after you see an action.

- Use a variety of affirmation methods:

  — spoken—compliments to them, compliments to others in their hearing

  — written—notes, screen-saver messages, e-mails

  — physical—hugs, pats, extra privileges

Self-Designed Stationery

(see page 78)

Chapter 5

Does Anybody Else Out There Have Teenagers?

Connect Parents with Each Other

"Little do parents realize that the parents they compare themselves to feel just as vulnerable and wish they weren't alone in their frustrations."

"Many parents are as shy and socially awkward as the teenagers they parent."

"We offer another round of hot drinks and let casual conversation take over."

The triangle (bottom to top): ACKNOWLEDGE, AFFIRM, COMMUNICATE, ENCOURAGE, 5 CONNECT, EQUIP, INVOLVE, EDUCATE, CO-NURTURE

On many days parents of teens feel as if they're the only parents in the world who are dealing with the issues they face at home. They often blame themselves and assume they're alone in the struggles they have with their kids.

- "Am I the only parent on the planet who is so incompetent that I can't get my nearly adult children to make their own beds or pick up their underwear?"

- "Is there any other mom in the world like me who's forced to learn the language of grunts and groans to understand a teen?"

- "Is mine the only car on the block that comes back with fast food trash and an empty gas tank whenever my kids have borrowed it?"

- "Don't any other parents in my community have any standards about where their kids can be after midnight? Are we really the only family in town with a curfew?"

- "Are any other dads out here on a Saturday morning mowing the lawn while three perfectly healthy teenagers sit inside playing Nintendo and enjoy a leisurely brunch after sleeping until 10:30?"

The feeling of being "the only one" can be a powerful discourager for many parents. When parents pretend everything is fine in their families (which may be especially true of church families), parents often feel they're struggling with their kids because they aren't parenting correctly. Little do parents realize that the parents they compare themselves to feel just as vulnerable and wish they weren't alone in *their* frustrations.

We can't assume parents are meeting each other and connecting, no matter how friendly the church might be. Most adults function with a relatively small circle of friends. Many are as shy and socially awkward as the teenagers they parent. Besides, the thought of making new friends often feels like a lot of work even though parents may recognize the benefits. When we present opportunities that build bridges between parents, we offer them the gifts of support and encouragement.

Notice that even at this fifth level in the parent ministry process, our role is in no way intrusive. We are not the experts, not "God's gift to parents." We are simply facilitators helping parents minister to one another. It's a humble role but an important one.

Why Parents Need to Be Connected

To Tap into Collective Wisdom
Proverbs 11:14 says, "For lack of guidance a nation falls, but many advisors make victory sure." Facilitating parent-to-parent relationships allows them to benefit from the larger pool of parenting wisdom that exists in every community. Parents of teenagers experience many firsts with their kids, so finding a parent who has dealt with a certain situation before can be invaluable. My wife and I have raised a son who has a learning disability. Many times we've leaned on the wisdom and experiences of other parents who have been in similar circumstances

To Have a Place to Share What They've Learned
When parents are going through difficult times with their children, they often ask themselves what good could possibly come out of the situation. Even minor skirmishes can be a laboratory for important lessons. Parents are usually open to sharing lessons they've learned, which often happens informally as they relate to other parents and explore one another's stories. Sometimes sharing takes place when we give parents the opportunity to publicly tell their stories or pair them up in monitored mentoring relationships.

Paul illustrates this concept in 2 Corinthians 1:4 when he praises "the God of all comfort who comforts us in all our troubles, so that we can comfort those in any trouble with the comfort we ourselves have received from God." What a wonderful picture of parents connecting with each other for the sake of mutual ministry.

To Develop a Balanced Perspective
As has already been stated, the years of parenting adolescents can be filled with anxiety. Because of the newness of their experiences, many parents just don't have a good sense of what's normal. When they don't have other parents to talk to, it's easy for parents to assume that their family is atypical, that their kids are nuts, that they're the worst parents on the planet (other than sea turtles who plant their eggs on the beach to go surfing, leaving the little guys to figure out the way to the water). When parents get a chance to talk with other parents about their feelings, fears, and frustrations, they often walk away feeling a huge sense of relief: "Someone else has the same hopeless feelings I do."

Parents who are connected with other parents have substantial advantages over those who parent in isolation. It may be one of the reasons so many parents find themselves reconsidering the place of church in their lives when their kids hit junior high.

Connecting Parents

Ranesha, Meet Elena

Simply introducing parents to one another at every opportunity we have is a great start to the connection process. Some adults are outgoing enough to get to know new people, but many are uncomfortable with more than a superficial, "Hi. How are you?" As we get to know parents, we'll develop a sense of who they might naturally connect with. Think about interests parents might have in common as a starting point for conversation.

- similar backgrounds
- kids who are friends
- neighborhoods
- sports affinities
- hobbies and leisure pursuits
- other interests

All of these are great connecting points that a thinking matchmaker can highlight when introducing people. Use opportunities before and after church or make it a point to attend adult events (men's or women's meetings, prayer meetings, etc.) where you can concentrate on connecting parents without students vying for your attention.

Featured Family

Each week feature one family by—

- Posting a picture and family biography (see **Family Portrait** on page 96) on your bulletin board. As you can see, the questions offer opportunities for parents to find common ground.

- Introducing the featured family during the worship service. Have them stand or project their photo when introduced. Highlight a few details from their Family Portrait. Encourage others to greet them after the service.

You Pray for My Kid, and I'll Pray for Yours

Invite parents to partner with one another in intercessory prayer for their teens. Parents can be in touch with each other on a weekly basis to share requests and answers to prayer. You may find the program most effective if you pair up two moms or two dads but other options are to throw all the participants' names in a hat or to assign secret prayer partners. Use **Prayer Partner Parents** (page 97) as a way of gathering the information you'll need to put the pairs together. Establish new partnerships each year.

Name Tag Wisdom

In a rush to get ready for a parent event, I didn't set up the printing for name tags correctly. I intended to use large, bold letters declaring the parent's name and smaller, lightweight letters indicating the teen's name, but my computer misread the information in my database (that's how it seems to me) and reversed the information on the name tags. After I saw what happened, I decided to go with the result to see how the change would work. It was one of those mistakes that ends up working better than the original plan! The kid's names become a quick point of identification and an instant conversation starter.

Sunday Night Connections

I first tried this idea on Sunday evenings; hence the name. Pick any evening that works for you and the parents in your community, and change the name accordingly.

We invited about a dozen parents to our home for a simple dessert with the aim of inviting all the parents over the course of several months. We made sure to have a mix of couples and singles as well as church and community parents. In each group a few parents usually knew each other, but many of them didn't know anyone. After everyone had a mug of coffee or hot chocolate in hand, we gathered in one room where we introduced ourselves by way of answering several simple questions:

- What's your name?

- What are the names and ages of your teens?

- Where did you go to high school?

- What are two or three words you'd use to describe your family during your teenage years?

- What's one lesson you hope your kids will learn earlier in life than you did?

Notice the absence of questions related to marital status, employment, education, and other potentially divisive topics. The focus was that we're all parents of teens. After the intros I opened the floor for questions about the youth ministry program, suggestions for improvements, and, finally, for ways we could pray for parents or teens. In virtually every group the prayer request time became a significant connecting point for parents.

We offered another round of hot drinks and let casual conversation take over. Each evening , we discovered that people were reluctant to leave, and relationships were formed.

Christmas Cookie Exchange

A fun, festive (and almost no-work) way for you to host parents in your home is a Christmas cookie exchange. Pick a Sunday afternoon around Christmas, send out invitations, vacuum your house or apartment, throw a few cinnamon sticks in the apple juice to make parents think you have cider, pop in the Boney M Christmas CD, and wait for parents to show up so they can connect with each other.

On the invitation ask everyone to bring three dozen cookies (baked or bought—but no cheapies). Let them munch up to a dozen cookies while they're connecting. Then, as they leave, they can help themselves to a mixed couple of dozen to take home.

The bonus is that almost nobody ever eats a dozen, so you have tons of leftover cookies when the last parent walks out the door. Everyone wins!

Parent Only and Intergenerational Events

Plan a few social events throughout the year that are open to parents only—or look for events already on your calendar that are suitable for parents and teens to attend together.

One event our students always enjoy is Do It Yourself Mini Golf Night. In teams of three to five, they design and build a miniature golf hole in one of the Sunday school rooms or hallways of the education wing. On Friday night they install their masterpieces and golf a round or two. Since they like to see what their kids put together, have parents come on Saturday night to play the course.

Guess Whose Parents Are Coming to Dinner?

Ask about 20 to 25 percent of your parents to host a dinner party at their home for other parents. (If you have 25 families, get five or six host homes.) Your most supportive parents are a good place to start—but make sure they can cook!

Have the others show up at the church 30 minutes before dinner with their best dessert. In a simple or elaborate ceremony, have parents pick a map out of a chef's hat. The map indicates where they'll be going to dinner. The hosts have no idea who'll be showing up, and the guests don't know where they're going—until the last minute.

Invite everyone back to the church at a designated time for dessert. Throw in a closing mixer to finish up the evening.

Parents Only Fundraiser

Appoint a committee of parents to organize a surprise fundraiser to support the missions trip or service project your students are planning. Connect parents through car washes, any number of "athons," or slave auctions (parents with special abilities—carpenters, computer programmers, auto mechanics, bakers—auction their services to the highest bidder). Parents get to know each other, and the activities give them a chance to support the kids.

Parent Appreciation Banquet

Let students plan a Parent Appreciation Banquet. They can set up the room, prepare the food, and create the program. Make it a quality night. Invite the parents for hors d'oeuvres before dinner. If you have musicians in your group, serve the appetizers in a room set up like a classy piano bar.

Use a maitre d' to seat parents for dinner. Students can serve the tables where their parents are seated. After dinner you can express appreciation for the support of the parents throughout the year and perhaps emcee a lighthearted award ceremony for parents who have been specially involved. The highlight of the evening is when the students give each of their parents a letter they've written (at a previous youth group activity) to say thanks.

Formal Connections between Parents

Parent-to-Parent Mentoring

After you've worked with families for a while, you'll have relationships with a growing group of parents whose kids have graduated from your ministry. Many are wise parents whose expertise and experience could be helpful to parents with young teen years. The mentoring parents typically should be at least 10 years older than the younger parents so a natural respect and appreciation will develop for what the mentors have learned along the way.

Begin by asking mature, experienced parents to be mentors. When you have some mentors lined up, offer the ministry to younger parents. Whether you make the offer individually or publicly depends on how many mentors are available.

A great way to kick off the Parent-to-Parent Mentoring Program is to host a parenting Q&A night with a panel of "experts" who have already seen their kids through the wonderful teenage years. The parents who are available as mentors will be your panel. See **A Panel of Parenting Wisdom** (page 111) for details.

Be sure you have carefully defined what the expectations are for both sets of parents. See **Parent-to-Parent Partnership** (page 98-99) for a sample. You may want to offer mentoring only to parents whose kids are in their first year of your group. Then mentors can work with a new family each year, limit their commitment to the other parents, and can opt out for a year if they need to.

Support for Hurting Parents

In the course of parenting adolescents, many families experience specific types of pain—an eating disorder, a suicide, an attempted suicide, a runaway, a pregnancy, an accidental death of a teenager, an arrest, or any number of other challenges. Some parents never recover from the devastation. But others find grace to rise above the circumstances. Their experience is a resource worth tapping.

As healing occurs and parents are willing to share their progress with you, it's appropriate to ask if they might be willing—when they're ready—to talk with other parents experiencing similar circumstances. This support ministry is not meant to be public. It happens behind the scenes as you quietly connect parents who have common experiences.

• • •

FROM COMFORT TO COMFORT

In the opening section of this chapter, you read from 2 Corinthians 1 in which Paul writes about using the comfort we've received to provide comfort to others. Notice the principle of this passage: *out of our comfort* we comfort others.

Some folks have the idea that we can minister to others out of our *pain*. Certainly our shared pain gives rapport and understanding, but our comfort from Christ gives us the foundation for ministry.

Be careful to not simply bring together parents who have the same sort of pain. They may have understanding but not be able to comfort each other yet. Look for parents who have tasted Christ's comfort; that will be the well from which their help for others will come.

We're All in This Together

A parent meeting to connect parents of teens with one another

Significant parent ministry can take place between parents They can encourage one another in ways nonparents simply cannot. A good youth worker will look for every opportunity to connect parents with one another. To make the event less awkward for single parents, some activities are designed for individuals.

The *Big* Picture

Offer parents a casual, lighthearted opportunity to get to know one another by discussing issues common to parents of teens. The guided conversation is designed to jumpstart mutually encouraging relationships.

Come On In!

You'll need...
- Nametags
- Pens or markers

Give people nametags as they come in. In addition to their own names, have them write their kids' names on the nametag as well.

Have the refreshments ready to go before people arrive, but don't serve them until after the first get-acquainted activity. If possible, have the room set with tables so groups can sit around them.

How Are Ya?

You'll need...
- Copies of **Totally Awesome** (page 100), one for each group
- Pens, one for each group

Ask people to move into groups of five to seven per table. Request that spouses sit at different tables. Give each group a copy of **Totally Awesome** (page 100) and a pen Have them calculate the group's average score. Let the group with the *lowest* average score head for the refreshment table first. Dismiss the other groups in order of increasing averages.

When parents have gotten refreshments, have them go back to their tables for a quick trip back to their own teenage years.

The Good Old Days

You'll need...
- Copies of **Good Old Days** (page 101), one for each group

While people are getting their snacks, place a copy of **The Good Old Days** (page 101) on each table. While people are munching on their snacks, parents can tell memorable stories to their group from one of the categories. After they've told one story, they can continue with additional tales until you call time.

Give the groups an idea of the time limit for the activity (or per story) so they make sure everyone gets a turn. This activity is simply to help them kickstart their conversations and to get to know other parents.

Thumbs Up, Thumbs Down

Explain that you are going to read some statements. If they agree with the statement, they signal thumbs up (high so everyone can see). If they disagree they signal thumbs down. They then move into groups of four or five people in which both opinions are represented (that is, at least one person in the group must agree and at least one person must disagree). Give them two minutes to explain their positions. Make sure the groups are mixing from statement to statement.

- When it comes to options and opportunities, the world is a better place for kids today than previous generations.
- Kids today are wiser and more sophisticated, not just more informed, than kids were 10 or 20 years ago.
- In general, this generation of kids is more emotionally healthy than we were at that age.
- How kids turn out has more to do with how God made them than how they've been parented.
- I've enjoyed parenting my kids as teenagers more than I did when they were preschoolers.
- It's more important for teenagers to do well socially than academically during the first two years of high school
- Parents of teenagers should make every effort to keep the family free of conflict.

The statements don't have correct answers; they're just another forum for parents to get to know one another.

I've Done *Something* Right!

You'll need...
- Copies of **I've Done *Something* Right!** (page 102), one for each group

Most parents are painfully aware of the mistakes they've made with their kids. They don't need to be reminded of missed opportunities, misplaced priorities, and miscommunicated messages. This activity is an opportunity for them to reflect on a few of their successes. Have people regroup, with spouses if they prefer.

Give parents an opportunity to share with their group on the topics listed on **I've Done *Something* Right!** (page 102). It's a great opportunity for parents to learn from one another without creating a formal teaching relationship.

What's a Parent to Do?

Read the following scenarios, one at a time. After each, have one parent volunteer to tell how he or she would respond. Let them know they only have three minutes for each response.

Your 13-year-old daughter has been elusive recently and you're concerned about that. She doesn't give straight answers to your questions about where she's going and who she's with. You're getting breakfast early one morning before work when you see your daughter's diary lying with its little key on the kitchen counter.

Your 17-year-old son is six months from high school graduation. He returns from a Christmas mission trip and tells you that God has called him into full-time missionary service, that he's come to realize how urgent it is to get the gospel to all people, and that he will not be going to college as planned when he graduates. Instead he is committed to going on a two-year assignment with the agency from the Christmas trip. He's hoping that it will turn into a full-time ministry.

Your 16-year-old daughter arrives home from school on the Thursday before the long week-end in May and announces that she's going camping with a group of kids for the next four days. Guys and gals are going, but your daughter says not to worry because no one is dating anyone else in the group and her friend's college-aged sister is coming to chaperone.

While moving your 14-year-old son's laundry from the washing machine to the dryer, you find a three-pack of condoms in the tangle of jeans, socks, and underwear.

Wrap up the activity by saying something like this—

Parenting teenagers obviously requires us to have wisdom beyond what most parents have. It's probably easier to come up with advice for other people than it is to handle some of the routine stuff that comes up in our own homes on a daily basis.

The good news is that we don't have to do this on our own. Listen to what God tells us in James 1:5: "If any of you lacks wisdom, he should ask God who gives generously to all without finding fault and it will be given."

Have parents take a few minutes to share (in their groups) about a specific area of parenting they know they need wisdom for right now. Have the groups pray together about the areas they've discussed or pray on behalf of all of the needs as you close the evening.

Remind people that the purpose of the evening was to get to know fellow parents. Encourage parents to stay for more refreshments or coffee and chat. Close in prayer.

A Family Portrait

(see page 89)

Attach or draw family photo here

Names (include ages or grades for the kids) ▶▶

◀◀ How long has your family been part of this church family?

What are the specific areas of church life where each of you is involved? ▶▶

◀◀ What neighborhood do you live in?

Where do the kids go to school? ▶▶

◀◀ Where else have you lived (other cities. states. countries)?

What was the best vacation your family has ever taken? ▶▶

◀◀ If your family had a free Saturday. what would you do for fun?

Tell about family pets (or pet peeves). ▶▶

◀◀ Name a hobby. sport. or special interest for each family member.

The Last Word
Tell us what we need to know to better understand your family. ▶▶

Prayer Partner Parents

(see page 89)

PARENT'S NAME	TEENAGER'S NAME
ADDRESS	ADDRESS
PHONE	PHONE
E-MAIL	E-MAIL

birthday _____

_____ grade in school

school _____

_____ attitudes about school

activities, hobbies, sports, job _____

_____ health or physical prayer needs

relational prayer needs _____

_____ spiritual prayer needs

parenting prayer needs _____

Parent-to-Parent Partnership

(see page 91)

Commitment to Mentor

Because...

I've experienced the sometimes hazardous path of parenting adolescents...
I've made more than my share of mistakes along the way...
I've realized there's no right or easy way to parent...
I've learned a few things (often the hard way)...
I've experienced the power of prayer...
I've survived... so far...

I have some sense of what you are experiencing...
I can pray for you with compassion...
I can empathetically listen to your experiences...
I can encourage you as you parent...
I can help you find hope...
I know you'll survive...

- Let's get to know each other better during the upcoming year.
- Let's walk together throughout this year seeking wisdom as parents.
- Let's meet at least monthly (at my initiative), so we can pray together and talk about our relationships with our young adult children.
- Let's read a book on marriage or family issues and discuss what we are learning.
- Let's pursue wisdom related to raising healthy teenagers in a rapidly changing world.

Here are my commitments to you:

- To pray for you and your family regularly.
- To share my parenting experiences with you honestly —my failures as well as my successes.
- To be available should a crisis arise.
- To challenge you in love, if I see behaviors that might be destructive to the well being of your family.
- To holding you accountable in areas that we together identify as needing development.
- To keep personal information in confidence.

_____
signature
Been there, done that

_____
signature
Haven't been there yet

Parent-to-Parent Partnership

(see page 91)

Commitment to Mentoring Relationship

Because...

You've experienced the sometimes hazardous path of parenting adolescents...
You've realized there's no right or easy way to parent...
You've learned a few things...
You've experienced the power of prayer...
You've survived... so far...

You have some sense of what I'm experiencing...
You can pray for me with compassion...
You can listen to my experiences...
You can encourage me as I parent...
You can help me find hope...
You know I'll survive...

- Let's get to know each other well during the upcoming year.
- Let's walk together throughout this year, seeking wisdom as parents.
- Let's meet at least monthly so we can pray together and talk about our relationships with our young adult children.
- Let's read a book on marriage or family issues and discuss what we are learning.
- Let's pursue wisdom related to raising healthy teenagers in a rapidly changing world.

Here are my commitments to you:

- To share prayer needs with you.
- To share my parenting experiences with you honestly —my failures as well as my successes.
- To turn to you should a crisis arise.
- To respond positively to your challenges in love, if you see behaviors that might be destructive to the well being of my family.
- To agree to be held accountable in areas that we together identify as needing development in me.
- To keep personal information in confidence.

_____   _____
signature   signature
Haven't been there yet   *Been there, done that*

Totally Awesome

(see page 93)

For this activity, "your children" include all biological, steps, and adopted children and children to whom you are the legal guardian, who are past their 11th birthday but have not yet reached their 20th as of today.

THE TOTAL AGES OF YOUR CHILDREN. _____

With January worth one point and December worth 12, _____ the value of the birth months of your children.

WITH BLONDE WORTH 5, BLACK WORTH 10,
BRUNETTE OR BROWN WORTH 15, RED WORTH 20,
AND ANY OTHER COLOR OR COMBINATION OF COLORS WORTH 25,
THE TOTAL HAIR COLOR SCORE FOR YOUR CHILDREN. _____

_____ Add the number representing the shoe sizes of your children.

Add 5 for every rodent, 10 for every bird, 15 for every cat, 20 for every dog, and 25 for reptiles, snakes or potbellied pigs that live as a pet at each house. _____

Subtotal _____

Divide the subtotal by the number of people in your group. This is your average.

=

_____

The Good Old Days

(see page 94)

Tell a memorable story from one of these categories. Keep your stories short so everyone has time to share. You can continue with additional tales if you have time.

sports

dating

pranks

CHURCH

school

POLICE

injuries

JObS

Share with your group from one of the following topics:

What's one thing you wouldn't change about the way you've parented your children?

What's a fun tradition in your family that everyone enjoys?

What's something you did with your kids when they were little that paid big dividends as they've grown up?

Tell about a time you gave your kid the benefit of the doubt and it proved to be the right thing to do.

What's a good rule you've had for the teenagers at your house?

How has having teenagers made you a better person?

Chapter 6

Give Them Some Tools and Everyone Wins

Equip Parents with Tools and Resources for the Parenting Task

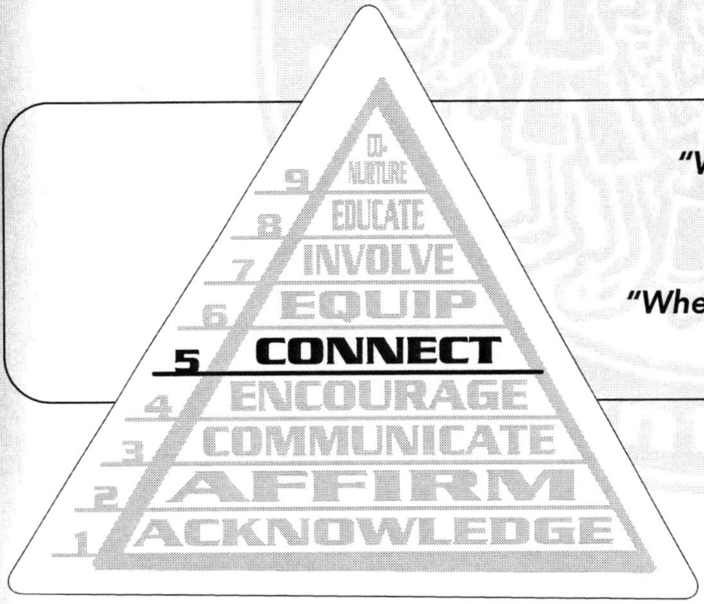
9 CO-NURTURE
8 EDUCATE
7 INVOLVE
6 EQUIP
5 CONNECT
4 ENCOURAGE
3 COMMUNICATE
2 AFFIRM
1 ACKNOWLEDGE

"When I'm doing a task for the first time, I feel like I can pull it off as long as I have the right tools."

"When it comes to media, the goal is thoughtful dialogue, not power struggles."

I'm a hardcore tool-time guy. There's nothing I love better than to wander the hardware aisles at Sears or Home Depot looking for the newest workshop gadget to help me with my current project. Over the years I've restored an old British sports car, built a cedar strip canoe, kept three or four motorcycles running, and renovated a house.

Projects like these are filled with joys, but the most frustrating moments come when I don't have the right tools to do the job. When I'm doing a task for the first time, I feel like I can pull it off as long as I have the right tools.

Parents often feel the same way. When they have the right tools, the parenting task always seems more manageable.

As youth workers we're familiar with the world of adolescents. We understand their music, their language, their relationships, and their unwritten rules. When we have rapport with their parents, we can put tools—information and resources—into their hands to help them manage their parenting jobs.

As we equip parents, we're simply giving them support in the job that we've consistently recognized as theirs. We're not evaluating their parenting or standing in judgment of their family. We're simply making available to them the kind of help they might benefit from, should they choose to take advantage of our offer.

In other words, even though we're moving toward the top of the parent ministry pyramid, we're not *intruding* into the family or assuming the role of expert when it comes to parenting adolescents. Remember, parents are often apprehensive of having their inadequacies exposed. If we approach them insensitively or arrogantly, we may lose future opportunities to minister to them and their kids. We've come a long way from acknowledging and affirming the family, but at no point in this process do we ever replace, upstage, or undermine parents in their role with their kids. We're giving them tools that will make them look good, even when we don't get any credit ourselves.

Here are some specific ideas you can use to equip parents for their job.

Events to Equip Parents

Panel of Experts

Every community has individuals with legitimate expertise in areas that affect families: youth division police officers and parole officers; schoolteachers, counselors, and principals; doctors; coaches; lawyers; and staff members of crisis pregnancy, suicide prevention, and mental health centers.

Consider hosting a panel discussion or Q&A evening that taps the expertise of these individuals on a topic of interest to parents. You're making expert resources available to parents instead of setting yourself up as the expert. Use **A Panel of Parenting Wisdom** (page 111) as a framework but adapt the ideas for these experts.

Understanding Your Teenager Seminar

You have two options for this idea. The first is to bring in the professional three-hour seminar "Understanding Your Teenager," delivered by veteran speakers (including me!) who are also parents of young adults. For more information, visit the Understanding Your Teenager Web site at gospelcom.net/uyt or call 800-561-9309. (The seminar is also available on video.)

The other option is to invite a local speaker who has developed good material on the subject. Have a clear idea of the speaker's presentation ability, the content the speaker will cover, and the perspective the speaker offers (such as supporting the role of parents).

Video-Based Parenting Classes

Several nationally known communicators have put their material on videotape with accompanying discussion questions and leader's guides. These video-driven sessions can be used in Sunday morning classes, on a parent retreat, or over the course of several evenings.

The beauty of this approach is that the expert is on tape, allowing parents to be more open to the material. Depending on the level of rapport you feel with the parents, you might consider having one of them facilitate the discussion. These cours-

VIDEO-BASED RESOURCES

Parenting Teenagers for Positive Results by Jim Burns (Group, 2001).

Parenting Adolescents by Kevin Huggins (NavPress, 1992).

Understanding Your Teenager: The Video by Wayne Rice (*Understanding Your Teenager* at www.uyt.com or 800-561-9309).

es can be effective outreach opportunities if you invite the parents of unchurched students or if parents bring neighbors and friends.

These videos can be expensive, so you might consider a shared purchase with another church or ministry.

Resources to Equip Parents

Family Central Resource Kiosk

Many churches have established a family resource center in the church library to make parenting tools readily accessible. Often church libraries are out of the main traffic flow and busy people may not get there. Raise the visibility of parenting resources to a new level by establishing a simple kiosk to keep these resources accessible and circulating.

Pattern your kiosk after the merchandising carts that have become popular at shopping malls. If you make a cabinet with locking curtains or shutters (or a volunteer does it for you), it can be closed up when the church is not in use and easily supervised before and after events. Display books, videos, pamphlets, and cassette tapes of workshops, seminars, or relevant radio programs.

Encourage parents to look through their homes for suitable material and to pick up taped messages or seminars from events they attend that may be added to the collection.

Library Resources for Parents of Adolescents

My suggested book list is presented in alphabetical order. About a dozen books, identified in bold text, are basic to a parent ministry library. Some listed books are published by secular organizations and may include content that is offensive to some. (On the other hand, don't avoid material solely because it originates from a secular publisher. Some of their resources are excellent additions to your collection.) Excellent new resources become available frequently, so keep watch.

As with every resource you use, you should review books for appropriateness in *your* setting. You might be overwhelmed to read them all cover to cover, but at least review the table of contents, read the foreword, skim key chapters, and seek feedback from others you trust. Booksellers like Amazon.com often publish reviews. You can also ask parents to read and review resources for you.

The 7 Habits of Highly Effective Families: Building a Beautiful Family Culture in a Turbulent World by Stephen R. Covey and Sandra Merrill Covey (Covey Leadership Center, 1997).

8 Simple Rules for Dating My Daughter and Other Tips from a Beleaguered Father (Not That Any of Them Work) by Bruce Cameron (Workman, 2001).

Age of Opportunity; A Biblical Guide to Parenting Teens (second edition) by Paul David Tripp (Presbyterian & Reformed Publishing, 2001).

All Grown Up and No Place to Go: Teenagers in Crisis (revised edition) by David Elkind (Perseus Press, 1997).

And Then I Had Teenagers; Encouragement for Parents of Teens and Preteens by Susan Alexander Yates (Baker, 2001).

Are We Having Fun Yet? The 16 Secrets of Happy Parenting by Kay Willis and Maryann Bucknum Brinley (Warner Books, 1997).

Bringing Up Parents: The Teenager's Handbook by Alex J. Packer (Free Spirit, 1992).

Cleared For Takeoff: 50 Ways Parents Can Help Their Teenagers Grow Up, Out, and Into a Life of Their Own by Wayne Rice (Word, 2000).

Courageous Parenting: The Passionate Pursuit of Your Teen's Heart by David Hutchins (NavPress, 2000).

(Continued...)

A Fine Young Man: What Parents, Mentors and Educators Can Do to Shape Adolescent Boys into Exceptional Men by Michael Gurian (J. P. Tarcher, 1999).

The Five Love Languages of Teenagers by Gary Chapman (Northfield, 2001).

Get Out of My Life but First Could You Drive Me and Cheryl to the Mall? by Anthony E. Wolf (Noonday Press, 1992).

Grounded For Life?! Stop Blowing Your Fuse and Start Communicating by Louise Felton Tracy (Parenting Press, 1994). *Helping the Struggling Adolescent: A Guide to Thirty-Six Common Problems for Counselors, Pastors, and Youth Workers (updated and expanded)* by Les Parrot (Zondervan, 2000).

How to Really Love Your Teenager by Ross Campbell (Victor Books, 1993).

Katie.com: My Story by Katherine Tarbox (Plume, 2001).

Living in a Step-Family without Getting Stepped On by Kevin Leman (Thomas Nelson, 1994).

The Myth of Maturity; What Teenagers Need from Parents to Become Adults by Terri Apter (W. W. Norton, 2001).

Parenting 911: How to Safeguard and Rescue Your 10- to 15-Year-Old from Substance Abuse, Depression, Sexual Encounters, Violence, Failure in School, Danger on the Internet, and Other Risky Situations by Charlene C. Giannetti and Margaret Sagarese (Broadway Books, 1999).

Parenting Adolescents by Kevin Huggins (NavPress, 1992).

Parenting Clues for the Clueless by Christopher D. Hudson, ed. (Promise Press, 1999).

Parenting Isn't for Cowards by James C. Dobson (Word Publishers, 1987).

Parenting Teens with Love and Logic: Preparing Adolescents for Responsible Adulthood by Foster Cline and Jim Fay (NavPress, 1993).

Parenting Today's Adolescent: Helping Your Child Avoid the Traps of the Preteen and Teen Years by Dennis Rainey and Barbara Rainey (Thomas Nelson, 1998).

Raising a Teenager: Parents and the Nurturing of a Responsible Teen by Jeanne Elium and Don Elium (Celestial Arts, 1999).

Raising Adults: Getting Kids Ready for the Real World by Jim Hancock (Pinon Press, 1999).

Real Boys: Rescuing Our Sons from the Myths of Boyhood by William Pollack (Owl Books, 1999).

Reclaiming Our Prodigal Sons and Daughters: A Practical Approach to Connecting With Youth in Conflict by Scott Larson (National Education Service, 2000).

Restoring the Teenage Soul: Nurturing Sound Hearts and Minds in a Confused Culture by Margaret J. Meeker (McKinley and Mann, 1999).

Reviving Ophelia: Saving the Selves of Adolescent Girls by Mary Pipher (Ballantine, 1995).

Surviving Your Adolescents: How to Manage and Let Go of Your 13-18 Year Olds by Thomas W. Phelan (Child Management, 1998).

Teens in Turmoil by Carol Maxym and Leslie B. York (Penguin Books, 2001).

Teen Tip: A Practical Survival Guide for Parents with Kids 11 to 19 by Tom McMahon (Pocket Books, 1996).

The Second Family: How Adolescent Power Is Changing the American Family by Ron Taffel (St. Martin's Press, 2001).

The Shelter of Each Other: Rebuilding Our Families by Mary Pipher (Ballantine, 1996).

A Tribe Apart: A Journey into the Heart of American Adolescence by Patricia Hersch (Ballantine, 1999).

Uncommon Sense for Parents with Teenagers by Michael Riera (Celestial Arts, 1995).

Understanding Today's Youth Culture by Walt Mueller (Tyndale, 1999).

Understanding Your Teenager by Wayne Rice and David Veerman (Word Books, 1999).

What Makes Your Teenager Tick? by G. Keith Olson (Group, 1988).

Why Can't We Talk: What Teens Would Share If Parents Would Listen by Michelle Trujillo (Health Communications, 2000).

Buy It, Read It, Share It

The cost of providing a steady stream of new resources for parents can be daunting. Keep your library current by encouraging families to purchase resources and donate them.

The trick to making this program work is to buy six to 10 resources yourself and display them in the parenting resource center or the library with the suggestion for a parent to make a donation to cover its cost. The purchaser is free to take the resource home with the understanding that they will return it the library or resource center in 30 days so it can be put into circulation for other parents to use.

In most cases the contributions can be handled as a *bona fide* donation to the church, since the only benefit the parent receives is being the first to borrow it.

You'll have less than $200 tied up in inventory while you're waiting for the resources to be adopted. See page 105-106 for a list of current resources for your parent ministry collection.

Video Documentaries

Adolescent and family issues are hot news topics. Every few weeks it seems that one of the major networks is airing a documentary or investigative report on some aspect of adolescence or family life. These programs are almost always available from the networks for a nominal fee. (A quick trip to the network Web site will give you the information you need to order them.) Make these video resources available to parents through your resource kiosk.

The problem with network programming is that they typically present a problem without solutions. Here's the chance for you to take the program to a new level. Create a discussion guide to go with the video that leads parents and their kids to discuss solutions or responses to the problem. Documentaries can lead to great discussion in the home if parents get a little help with the kinds of questions to ask.

Other Tools for Parents

Clip and Save

Newspapers and magazines are filled with tidbits that help parents understand youth culture and other issues related to their families. It might be a chart, recent research, perhaps a quote, or a whole article that's worth keeping. When you come across helpful information, it's good to get in the habit of clipping it or copying it for your files. Many youth workers already do that.

But how about passing it on to parents in an occasional insert for your parent newsletter or as a special mailing or hand-out on its own? It doesn't take a lot of time, but it does two things for you: it shows parents you're thinking about them, and it gives them valuable information to strengthen them in their task of parenting.

Keep these tips in mind:

- Find an avid newspaper reader and a news magazine reader and ask them to be your "clipper." I had a retired librarian on the lookout. She handed me a folder full of articles every two weeks. What a help!

- Be careful to include some upbeat information, or you might find yourself needing to change the name of your handout to "More Dismal Evidence That Parents Aren't Doing the Job." The media tends to report more bad news than good, so you might have to look hard for material that balances your content in each issue.

- Include an article, graph, or stat that is a good discussion starter and suggest parents talk about it with their kids during a meal. Write a few thought-provoking discussion questions to get them started.

- Don't overlook local information. Stats from your local school board, information about events in your community, and the perspective of local reporters and researchers makes the information even more relevant.

- Start a good filing system to organize your clipping treasures. **Youth Ministry Management Tools** (Youth Specialties, 2001) contains an excellent plan for a filing system. It will make your file drawer look like you should be the administrative pastor.

Worth Watching

Skim the television programming guide for the week and identify documentaries, talk shows, or prime time pieces of particular interest to parents. Post the info on the parent ministry bulletin board or on your parent ministry Web site to encourage people to tune in. Be selective in what you recommend and keep the board updated.

WEB-BASED MEDIA REVIEWS

- Center for Parent/Youth Understanding at www.cpyu.org. Located throughout the site in newsletters and articles, and in the Bulletin Board and Culture Facts.

- The Dove Foundation: www.dove.org. Contains reviews of movies, videos, and video games including sex, language, violence, drugs, nudity, and the occult.

- Family Style Film Guide: www.familystyle.com. Movie and video reviews, including ratings on profanity, nudity, sex, violence, and drugs/alcohol.

Media Watch

Several organizations have committed themselves to posting reviews of movies, newly released videos, video games, and TV shows on their Web sites. They are easily downloadable and can be made available to parents by way of Web site links, the parent ministry bulletin board, or on small fliers. Most of them give straightforward information about basic plotline, language, violence, sexual content, and other areas of concern. This information can help families make wise decisions about their media intake.

Be careful to present this service in a positive light by assuming your teens care about what they watch. If it becomes a basis for parents to get into fights with their kids about what they're watching, it will only lead to negative experiences for everyone. When it comes to media, the goal is thoughtful dialogue, not power struggles.

Link to Help

Here are a number of organizations committed to supporting families:

The National Center for Fathering
P. O. Box 413888
Kansas City, MO 64141
(800) 593-DADS
(913) 384-4661
fathers.com

Stepfamily Association of America, Inc.
650 J Street, Suite 205
Lincoln, NE 68508
(800) 735-0329
saafamilies.org

The Center for Parent/Youth Understanding
Walt Mueller
P. O. Box 414
Elizabethtown, PA 17022
(717) 361-8429
cpyu.org

Understanding Your Teenager
Wayne Rice
P. O. Box 420
Lakeside, CA 92040
(800) 561-9309
gospelcom.net/uyt

Family Dynamics Institute
P. O. Box 211668
Augusta, GA 30917
(800) 650-9995
(706) 855-9900
familydynamics.net

Focus on the Family
Dr. James Dobson
Colorado Springs, CO, 80995
(800) 232-6459
family.org

realFamilies
Dr. Kevin Lehman
P. O. Box 777
Wexford, PA 15090
realFamilies.com

Family Research Council
801 G Street, NW
Washington, DC 20001
(202) 393-2100
frc.org

• • •

A Panel of Parenting Wisdom

A parent meeting to tap the experience of veteran parents

This parent meeting is relatively simple, but it may be one of the most effective events you'll ever put together. It has potential to connect and encourage parents while it equips them for their roles as the spiritual nurturers of their children.

The *Big* Picture

This meeting gives parents a chance to benefit from the collective wisdom of a panel of veteran moms and dads.

Advanced Prep

> **You'll need...**
> - 5 to 7 panelists, chosen in advance
> - Copies of **Parent Panelist Perplexing Propositions** (page114), mailed in advance
> - A banner, as described, optional
> - Tables and chairs, for the panelists
> - Name cards, for the panelists
> - Microphones, optional

The secret of success for this meeting is to find parents for the panel who are finished raising their teenagers but who haven't lost touch with the world of teens—which translates to credibility. Choose parents representing a range of personalities and parenting styles and, of course, people who will be spontaneous and animated in sharing. Obviously you'll want a mix of moms and dads, singles and couples. Shoot for five to seven panelists. More are tough to manage; fewer may not give you the breadth of perspectives you want.

At least a week before the event, mail copies of **Parent Panelist Perplexing Propositions** (page 114), so panelists can prepare thoughtful answers. You probably won't have time to have each panelist share on every question, so make sure they understand that they do not have to answer questions they're not comfortable addressing or if they feel they have little to share.

A fun way to emphasize the depth of experience on your panel is to hang a banner behind the panelists with the total years of parenting experience. You might write PANEL OF PARENTAL EXPERIENCE: 139 YEARS OF FAMILY LESSONS LEARNED THE HARD WAY.

Set up tables for the panelists to sit at. Make large readable name cards for each person. If you are expecting a large group of parents, have several movable mikes at the tables and a mike out in the audience for questions.

Every good panel discussion has a moderator to keep the discussion moving along and to keep one panelist from dominating, and to call on audience members for questions. It's an appropriate role for the lead youth worker or youth pastor to take, or the job can be given to a respected parent.

I'd Like You to Meet...

You'll need...
- Family information and anecdotes, for each panelist
- Photos of the panelists' families, optional
- Projection system, optional

Begin the evening by thanking the panel for participating and introducing each one. Give their names, the names and ages of their kids, and interesting anecdotes or little-known facts (like Alex Trebeck on *Jeopardy*, only make the atmosphere more relaxed).

If your room is equipped appropriately, add dimension to the introductions by projecting a photo of the panelist's family during the introduction.

No Right Answer

You'll need...
- 6 sheets of heavy paper for each panelist
- 1 large dark marker for each panelist

This short warm-up validates the variety of opinions the panelists represent and the freedom each has to express them. Give each panelist six sheets of paper and a marker. As soon as you read them a question from the list below, have them write the first answer that comes to mind. Have them hold up their answers all at once. Make a brief comment about extremes or unusual answers, but don't get into discussions about answers. This is just a quick little ice breaker, so move through the activity quickly.

- What's the best age for a teenager to start dating?
- How much allowance should a 16-year-old girl who buys her own clothes get?
- What's a good curfew for a 14-year-old on Friday night?
- Looking back, what would you say is the ideal number of months between the births of kids?
- At what age should a child be able to make his or her own decision about church attendance?
- How many hours per week should kids be expected to do chores around the yard or house?

Priming the Pump

You'll need...
- 1 copy of **Parent Panelist Perplexing Propositions** (page 114)

Get the discussion off to a good start by asking several questions from **Parent Panelist Perplexing Propositions** on page 114.

And the Crowd Went Wild

You can get questions from the audience two ways.

The first is to have parents ask their questions directly to the panel or to a specific panel member. Often a comment a panelist makes will spark a follow-up question, request for clarification, or related inquiry. This method keeps the discussion lively. The problem with this method is that some people can monopolize the

WISE WORDS

Panel discussions have the potential to be energizing and fun or to be ponderously slow and redundant.

The most important thing the moderator can do is *keep it moving!*

Don't let every panelist speak to every issue. Cut folks off if they start to ramble. Remind the audience throughout the discussion that you won't be able to tap all the wisdom that exists on every topic. Draw out the panel members that you know have something to contribute. It's the moderator's responsibility to keep the audience engaged. Have fun!

Thank the panelists with a written note during the week following your event. A gift certificate to a restaurant or coffee stand is appropriate if your budget can handle it.

Thank you!

floor by rambling, telling meaningless stories about their own kids, and so on.

The alternative is to give parents paper to write down their questions. The moderator collects the questions. Not only are questions asked concisely, but also people can ask questions anonymously, the MC can group questions on similar themes, and, most importantly, the MC can eliminate inappropriate questions ("I guess we're all out of time for tonight!").

It's a Wrap

Serve refreshments at the end of the evening to give parents time to mingle. Encourage people to ask panel members specific questions that may have been too personal or that went unanswered for lack of time.

Make sure panel members know ahead of time that they're free to pray with people and deal with specific issues during this part of the meeting. Let them be pastors in the true sense of the word.

Parent Panelist Perplexing Propositions

(see page 112)

- As you look back on your years as a parent, have the teenage years been easier or tougher than you thought they would be? How?

- What's the most fun you've experienced as the parent of teenagers?

- In what area would you have been stricter with your teens? In what area might you have been more relaxed?

- What was the biggest challenge in nurturing your teenagers spiritually?

- Some people say that around their 13th or 14th birthday sweet and co-operative kids morph suddenly and without warning into unrecognizable monsters. What was your experience?

- What are the key differences you've found between raising teenage boys and teenage girls?

- What are some family traditions you've implemented that your teenagers have enjoyed?

- What's been your scariest moment as the parent of a teenager?

- What's a good rule your family has had and what consequences have you used for violating the rule?

- How did you handle allowances and money, purchasing clothes, entertainment expenses, and so forth?

- What's was the biggest surprise you experienced in raising teenagers?

- If you had it all to do over again, what would you do differently?

- What advice would you like to give parents just starting out with teenagers?

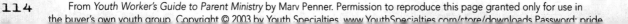

Chapter 7

Beyond Bringing Cookies and Driving the Van

Involve Parents in Your Youth Ministry

CO-
NURTURE
9
8 EDUCATE
7 **INVOLVE**
6 EQUIP
5 CONNECT
4 ENCOURAGE
3 COMMUNICATE
2 AFFIRM
1 ACKNOWLEDGE

"Think about weekly, monthly, or seasonal rhythms as you match jobs and willing workers."

"How much salami do you buy for 243 sandwiches?"

You've built a strong foundation for your ministry to parents by acknowledging parents' existence, affirming parents to their kids, committing yourself to communicating with parents, and being a constant encourager to parents. You've helped them build relationships with each other through connecting strategies, and you've provided resources to use in their relationships with their own kids.

Now it's time to get parents actively involved in achieving the broader goals of the youth program. Obviously every level up to this point in the parent ministry strategy represents some form of involvement, but this chapter takes it to a new level by identifying ways for parents to participate with you in a program specifically directed toward youth.

Involving as many parents as possible—at some level—will give parents a sense of shared ownership in the programs in which their sons and daughters participate. For many parents participation is an important step toward feeling like co-nurturers with you of their children.

Of course, not all parents will be involved in the same way nor to the same degree—nor should you expect them to be. Some parents are natural youth leaders and should be given an official platform from which to minister (with some important cautions we'll consider). Others will make their most significant contribution in less visible support roles. Some parents can be involved only occasionally, while others have greater flexibility in their schedules and can be counted on consistently. **A lot of parental involvement happens informally and may not be easily recognized, but all parental involvement makes an impact on the overall health of the ministry.**

Figure 7.1. Levels of Parental Involvement.

upfront and frequent

input and direction

occasional and specific

behind the scenes and supportive

informal and unofficial

Take a look at Figure 7.1, Levels of Parental Involvement. Notice the increasing levels of commitment and accountability from the outer ring to the center of the diagram.

The goal of your ministry should not be to have all parents move toward increasing levels of involvement. Some—by virtue of schedules, gifts, or other limiting factors (most notably, teens who don't want parents there)—will tend to be at the outer levels of involvement. That's fine. You need volunteers at each level of involvement to provide a good balance of support and ministry. The most important aspect of parental involvement is to let parents know you have a way for everyone to get involved in ways that work for them.

Levels of Involvement

Informal and Unofficial

The heart of informal and unofficial ministry is good old-fashioned hospitality that should be happening in every Christian home with teenagers. A lot of parents are actively involved in the lives of their kids and the friends of their kids. They create spontaneous or informal ministry opportunities—in their homes, at their summer cabins, in conjunction with community events. It's the spur of the moment invitation to stay for dinner or the unplanned Saturday afternoon football game in the park that ends up moving into the basement for an evening of games and nachos.

The spirit that drives this sort of broadly based openness to teenagers is well worth nurturing. Affirm parents who make their homes welcoming to students. Help them understand the value of a network of families in which kids are safe and supervised. Encourage moms and dads to initiate student get-togethers even though they aren't official events of the youth ministry.

And let parents know their interaction with the teens in their homes is important. When it comes to raising teenagers, parents are encouraged to know that other parents in the church share concern for kids and appreciate providing a safe home for their kids to meet and socialize.

One danger of informal ministry is that exclusive groups will form. Encourage parents to encourage teens to invite a few new kids to the get-togethers to expand their circle of friends.

Many a young person will point to a spontaneous conversation with a friend's parent as a significant moment in their spiritual journeys. Those moments can't be planned, but when they happen, we're glad to be part of a bigger family. Whatever we do to facilitate ministry at this level will be positive for everyone involved.

Behind the Scenes and Supportive

Often you will have parents committed to the purposes and mission of your youth ministry, but they aren't comfortable with relational ministry. They have enough time in their schedules to give you help you can count on, but perhaps they are quiet, introverted, or young in the faith.

Many of the logistical and administrative jobs of youth ministry are perfect for volunteers who want to work behind the scenes. Think about weekly, monthly, or seasonal rhythms as you match jobs and willing workers—but be careful not to give responsibilities to adults that kids can handle.

Here are examples of how you can delegate support responsibilities:

- *Assist with office work.* Copy and collate lesson handouts, design brochures and event fliers, act as receptionist to the youth ministry department, keep filing up to date, assemble mailings, develop the weekly youth bulletin, finalize discussion questions for small group leaders based on your lesson or talk.

- *Research topics you will be teaching on.* Find information on the Internet or in commentaries, develop a list of appropriate scripture verses using a concordance, look for quotes or illustrations.

- *Assist with retreats or outreach events.* Search databases of games, themes, and activities; price and purchase prizes, costumes, and supplies; collect registrations and fees.

- *Keep the parent ministry bulletin board current.* Post movie reviews and articles, develop film and post photos, obtain family-of-the-week profiles. Change the bulletin board weekly and overhaul it monthly. (Let the kids manage the youth bulletin board—in keeping with the principle of having teens serve whenever appropriate.)

- *Download reviews.* Locate current movie, video, and television reviews for the parent bulletin board or newsletter.

- *Coordinate food.* Organize a team to provide refreshments. The coordinator doesn't have to provide all the refreshments, only make sure it's available. This eliminates a huge headache for those handling the relational ministry.

- *Provide childcare for other youth ministry volunteers.* Often young couples would be easier to recruit for hands-on ministry with teens if they didn't have to find sitters and pay for childcare.

- *Host small groups.* Offer a home where students and small group leaders can meet.

- *Clip articles, statistics, and other information of interest.* Search newspapers and magazines. Categorize clippings according to your filing system. Turn clippings in to you weekly.

- *Act as spiritual directors, mentors, prayer partners, and lay counselors.* People who freeze in front of a group may be excellent volunteers for one-on-one ministry.

- *Mentor or support parents on an individual basis.* A discussion of this ministry is found in Chapter 5.

Occasional and Specific

Some parents will help occasionally with specific tasks. The involvement is sporadic and unpredictable—and that's not necessarily a bad thing. Some parents have special skills or aptitudes that are beneficial for one-time projects related to their area of expertise (or their schedule doesn't allow currentfrontline ministry). Some youth workers insist on an all-or-nothing commitment and in the process may overlook gifted parents who could make great contributions.

Without question, consistent, committed volunteers are crucial to a stable ministry, but once that team is in place, it can be dramatically strengthened through the use of a diverse team of occasional workers.

Wherever possible, have students work along with the skilled adult so that mentoring can take place. Use gifted parents in areas such as:

- *Construction, electrical wiring, and painting.* When the youth room needs new storage cupboards or the kids want a skateboard ramp for outreach in the parking lot, it's a good idea to use volunteers who know what they're doing and have the tools for the project.

- *Sewing.* Use sewing volunteers when you need costumes for a drama, curtains for the youth room, or 12 bed sheets sewn together for a giant drive-in movie screen.

- *Training.* The sky's the limit in this category. Train students to run the sound board or video editor. Train teens to teach preschoolers. Train the mission-trip team to lay bricks. Train the musicians and singers to develop the worship experience. How about language training by a fluent speaker? Draw upon the expertise available to you whenever you need it.

- *Teaching.* Schedule a volunteer to teach a 3- or 4-week series in your Sunday school or weekly Bible study. We hosted three weeks titled Stump the Seminoid, a series with a dad who taught at a nearby seminary. He answered tough questions kids had about the Bible. Look for people who are knowledge-able about a particular topic: life of Christ, cults, the Old Testament, end times, etc.

- *Photography and video production.* Don't overlook students who can contribute in this area, but in some circumstances a professional video or photo shoot might be called for. Whenever possible, train a student.

- *Cooking and menu planning for retreats, lock-ins, daytrips, and special events.* How many youth workers know how much salami to buy for 243 sandwiches or how long to cook a 52-pound roast for the Valentine's banquet? Parents can help plan the menu, calculate the quantity, develop the logistics for cooking, shop for and deliver the food, and, when necessary, keep the bears away from the camp site. Some may simply be willing to provide the weekly snack on occasion.

- *Driving.* Using teenage drivers is a huge risk, no matter how confident they are. Use parents who own vans (or even smaller cars) to transport kids. Having a team of certified bus drivers allows you to super-vise students and keeps a lone certified driver from burning out.

- *Repairing machinery.* First aid for the church bus. Need I say more?

- *Speaking.* It could be in an area of specific expertise or just someone who's good at talking to students. Use these people as speakers on retreats or to give devotionals at special events. There may be a pro-fessional athlete, coach or community leader who would have something good to say to kids.

"He comes alongside us when we go through hard times and before you know it he brings us alongside someone else who is going through hard times so that we can be there for that person just like God was there for us."

2 Corinthians 1:3-4,
The Message

- *Story telling.* Ask parents who have unusual stories or backgrounds to share their testimonies with the kids. On one of our retreats, a couple who had made serious sexual mistakes told their story as part of a moral purity theme. If the speakers' kids attend, be sure they agree to have their parents involved.

- *Leading worship.* On a retreat or for a special opportunity of spiritual impact, a parent gifted in leading worship can provide variety from the usual leadership.

- *First aid.* Depending on the activity you're involved with—say, a remote mission trip—you might want to have a volunteer with medical training: a paramedic, EMT, nurse, or doctor come along with you. Not only does it give a parent with special training a chance to use it in ministry, but it helps other parents relax about their teens' well-being.

- *Lifeguard.* You can save a ton of money if you can avoid hiring a lifeguard for a retreat or pool party. (Some venues require you to have one.) More importantly, a lifeguard provides an extra measure of safety when you're planning a water-based event. If you ever have an emergency on a canoe trip or river-rafting ride, you'll be glad to have one along.

- *Organizing a special event.* Some parents might commit themselves to organizing a single event: a fundraiser, a banquet, or a service project, especially if it matches with their passion or special interest. Parents who can't commit to full involvement with youth ministry might be willing to take on a one-shot project.

- *Counseling.* As you become aware of parents' stories, you'll uncover experiences some students face (for example, alcoholic or abusive parents, suicide attempts, abortion, loss of family members, divorce, premarital sex). Some parents will develop a short-term relationship with a student to listen, encourage, guide, and pray. Lay counselors aren't intended to replace or be legitimate therapists, but they can walk alongside to offer compassion and empathy.

Input and Direction

In Chapter 3 you read about general communication principles for accurately informing parents about program details and carefully listening to their advice, concerns, and ideas. Every youth worker should be communicating with parents at that basic level.

Now let's take communication to a deeper level by looking at a formal process for parents to provide input and direction to your youth ministry program. Receiving parental feedback is critical in a ministry model that acknowledges parents as the key spiritual nurturers of their own children. The support that comes with a formal communication process can also make ministry much less lonely. As we move toward the goal of a co-nurturing partnership it becomes more important than ever to give parents a forum for involvement in shaping the purposes, components, and direction of the ministry.

A parents advisory council (PAC) is one of the best ways I know to get the feedback necessary for a growing, healthy partnership. Not only do you have an effective means of hearing from parents, but you also have an effective means of getting information back to parents.

Here are some ideas to consider when setting up a parents advisory council.

- Wait to establish a PAC; don't begin during your first year in a new ministry. It takes at least that long to identify parents with a genuine interest in supporting your ministry and those who have a personal agenda to impose on you. Some of the folks who are so eager to know you and who gush with their enthusiastic support in the first few months often end up being the last people you want in your inner circle of advisors and encouragers. During the first year talk and listen to as many people as possible to get an accurate picture of the players before you start picking your team.

- Unless your church has a constitutional mandate to the contrary, *appoint* or *invite* parents to your first council instead of electing them. Create a list of 10 to 15 individuals or couples. Run the list by a pastor or a trusted elder at your church who can warn you if any red flags pop up. The pastor or elder can help you determine the order in which you might want to approach people. Pray about whom to ask, with a goal of establishing a council of five to seven families (represented by either a single parent or a couple). This will typically give you a council of about 10 parents.

- Seek to develop a council that represents an accurate cross-section of youth ministry families. For instance, if you serve junior and senior high students, be sure your parent council reflects both. Include married and single parents, mothers and fathers, a variety of racial and ethnic groups. You might have other issues to balance in your particular circumstance: home-schoolers and traditional education, rural and town (or city) families. Try to include representatives from the natural groupings in your setting. Your council won't be perfect, but seek balance. You might even invite a supportive, unchurched parent to be part of the group. See **Sample Letter Inviting Parents to Join Your Parent Advisory Council** on page 132.

- Be sure the council understands their two-fold purpose (which goes beyond giving advice):

  — The council supports and represents the youth ministry to parents.
  — The council represents parents to the youth ministry.

Decide whether the council has legislative power or acts in an advisory capacity. And make sure parents understand the difference. If you want them to be advisors, but they see themselves as in-charge decision makers, you've got a problem! See **PAC Member Job Description** on page 131.

- Don't equate being on the parents advisory council with having to do all the work in the youth ministry. Certainly you want the council to set a good example of involvement, but they're primary role is to be a voice to and from the youth ministry. If they begin to sense that they're just cheap labor, you will find it much harder to replace them when they quit (which won't take long).

- Meet regularly but don't kill them with meetings. In most cases a quarterly meeting is sufficient. Perhaps twice a year will do. These people don't need more meetings—but they do need a voice. Between meetings stay in close touch with council members. Let them know that if they sense a need to call a meeting based on what they are hearing from other parents you'll make it a priority.

- Once the parent advisory council is established, *you should not* make any major decisions about the direction of the ministry or philosophy of ministry without engaging council members in discussion. A quick standup meeting after church to address a pressing decision could save a lot of grief in the long run.

- Introduce the council members during an all-parent meeting or parent appreciation dinner. Make a big deal of it. Let parents know that you take their involvement seriously. Distribute small cards or bookmarks with the names and phone numbers of the council members, so parents will know how to get in touch with their representatives.

- After the first group is established, allow them to discuss the issue of how they will replace themselves: through nominations and elections, suggestions from within the group, continued suggestions and invitations from the youth pastor, or other processes the member may suggest.

- Have the group identify a chairperson to share the leadership of the group with you. Having a co-chair is always helpful when a group's mandate is two-way communication.

- Consider having council members represent the youth ministry department on church boards and committees in which you want the "youth voice" to be heard.

- Be careful not to violate your church's charter or constitution by having a PAC. Talk to a knowledgeable individual before you take any action that might get you in trouble.

- You may want to establish a special or temporary PAC for a specific component of your ministry. For example, a youth choir that travels could be a major piece of your program. So could Bible Quiz or an upcoming missions trip.

The bottom line is to make sure that you're listening to parents carefully and that they're hearing you. Parents can be your best allies or your worst nightmare.

Upfront and Visible

Most youth ministries in the world are operated primarily by a group of committed adult volunteers: the people teaching the classes; leading the small groups; planning retreats, fundraisers, service projects, and special events; and, most importantly, building relationally into the lives of the students in their care. The work can be tough and taxing at times.

Many churches struggle to recruit enough adults to keep their youth programs viable. Parents seem like the perfect solution. Just like the parents of small children should take turns in the nursery, parents of teens should run the youth group—or so the theory goes.

But it's not quite that simple. Some parents are gifted as youth leaders. They have the patience and understanding to connect well with kids. They don't mind the chaos and the noise that comes with the job. They're willing to backpack into faraway places and eat badly cooked macaroni and cheese in the rain. But we all know that plenty of parents don't cut it with kids—often not even their own.

A balanced team of volunteers ideally will have diversity in gender, age, and background. Some parents may be represented, but the team may also include college students, younger married couples, and perhaps a grandparent or two. Involving parents as key youth leaders has benefits *and* dangers. Putting them into leadership simply because they're parents isn't wise.

The Benefits of Parents as Youth Group Leaders

- Parents may understand the world of teenagers—their issues, their music, their emotions, their friendships. It's the world their kids live in, so they aren't taken by surprise.

- Parents have a vested interest in a quality youth program, since their kids are the direct beneficiaries. Committed parents work hard to make sure the program is satisfying to their own kids and their kids' friends.

- When parents give their kids rides to and from events, they're already at the meetings. For them to stay and be involved isn't such an imposition.

- Many parents of teens don't need daycare or baby-sitting for other children. With leaders who have small children, childcare can be a big hassle.

- Parents often have a level of maturity and tempered perspective that comes from living with kids. You may find them more patient, understanding, and tolerant than younger leaders because they have more life experience.

- Some parents know the history and understand the politics of your church or community. They can save a teachable youth worker untold grief by being "inside" advisors.

- Parents can be advocates for the youth ministry department to the other parents they may be naturally connected to by virtue of being in a common age group.

- It's harder for them to say no when being recruited because they have a sense of obligation. Mind you, it's no fun to work with people who have responded out of obligation, but when it's all you've got…

The Down Side of Parents as Youth Group Leaders

- To state the obvious, parents are older than college students and young couples. That may mean being less flexible, less spontaneous, more set in their ways. Adolescents often see adults five to seven years older than themselves as ideal role models. Forty-year-olds don't always make the role-model cut.

- Parents may have their own agendas, rather than the group's best interest at heart. One parent volunteer in my ministry was so committed to her pet project that when the other team members disagreed with her about it, she angrily left the church.

- Some parents may have a hard time acting "normal" when their own kids are in the youth group. They may be too detached and, in their effort not to give their teens preferential treatment, ignore them altogether, or they over invest in their kids to the point where they may as well have stayed home and just played checkers together.

- You may have parents who see their role as being a critic or spy, sort of like the quality control officer. Instead of contributing to the health of the program, they hang back and evaluate.

- Often the kids of potential parent volunteers just don't want them there!

Involving Parents as Youth Group Leaders

- Before you start the recruitment process, ask your students—individually. When kids are negative or obviously cautious, don't move forward. It's not worth ruining a teenager's youth ministry experience. Be careful to distinguish between the normal reticence kids may have about doing anything with their parents and a clearly expressed aversion.

- Consider having parents work in the age group opposite from their children: in high school when their kids are in junior high or in junior high when their kids are in high school.

- When parents serve in the same age group as their children, consider setting up your small groups so that teens and their parents are separated.

- Be sure to monitor the arrangement regularly, talking with parents and kids (separately). If tensions emerge in the home, an unwillingness on the part of kids to attend when their parents are present, or if parents become uncomfortable, consider freeing them from their commitment.

• • •

Have Your Say

A parent meeting to gather input on youth ministry structure and direction

Youth workers who consider themselves servants supporting parents will welcome parental input in shaping youth ministry programs. Parents have a positive contribution to make. When you let parents have a say, you minimize the us-versus-them mentality.

The *Big* Picture

Give parents the opportunity to discuss the direction of the youth ministry program with you.

More or Less? It's a Changing World

You'll need...
- Copies of **Kids Today...** (page 128), one for each group
- Pens, one for each group
- Newsprint
- Markers
- Tape or pins

Help parents realize that kids live in a different world than they grew up in, mainly because the pressures are more intense.

Ask parents to agree or disagree with this statement and to give their reasons: *It's more or less the same being a teenager today as it was 25 years ago.* Most parents will disagree, although you may have a few who say that kids have always faced peer pressure, they've always had to cope with hormones, and they've always had drugs and alcohol to tempt them.

Have parents break into groups of five to seven and assign one person to be the secretary. Pass out a copy of **Kids Today...** (page 128) and a pen to each group. Ask the groups to brainstorm endings to each sentence. Give them an opportunity to draw generalizations (common features) about items on each lists (for example, destructive potential, moral losses, freedom from pain, etc.)

Distribute newsprint and markers. Have each group wrap up their discussion by writing answers to the following sentences:

- The single biggest need of teenagers in our church is...
- The single biggest need of teenagers in our community is...

These questions create a setting in which the needs of church and *community* kids are front and center. With guidance, later discussion may stay focused on ministry structure and programming priorities with less selfish and shallow input. Let each group post it's answers around the room.

Review the answers, and ask, "How are we doing as families and as a church at meeting these needs?" Allow people to give feedback.

Reiterate that the youth ministry team is committed to being relevant to the needs of both church and community kids and that the meeting is all about tapping the wisdom and experience of parents to make the ministry as meaningful as possible.

May I Have Your Order Please?

You'll need...
- Copies of **May I Have Your Order Please?** (page 129), one for each group
- Scissors
- Tape or pins

Many components can be built into a comprehensive youth ministry program. Find out which of these parents consider most important. Have people switch into new groups of four or five. Give each group a copy of **May I Have Your Order Please?** (page 129) and a pair of scissors.

Have them cut the page into strips and arrange the items in order of importance. Allow enough time for the groups to come to a consensus. When you sense the groups have settled on the order, give them a strip or two of tape to lay over the list as well as tape or pins to post it on the wall. You will undoubtedly have a variety of orders, but ask the whole group to identify commonly agreed upon high and low choices. Hopefully you'll find trends to focus direction for the rest of the meeting.

Help parents see that families have a variety of concerns, so that keeping the program balanced is a challenge.

If a particular component is clearly at the top of the list for everyone, ask for input on accomplishing more effectively.

Here's What Our Kids Really Need

You'll need...
- **Here's What Our Kids Really Need** (page 130), one for each person
- Pens, one for each person
- Newsprint
- Markers
- Tape or pins

Distribute **Here's What Our Kids Really Need** (page 130) and pens. Allow a few minutes for parents to pick their top five choices and rank them one to five. Encourage parents to include additional topics the might think of.

Ask parents to share their top-5 lists in groups of three. As you gather the lists, assure parents that you will tally the parent feedback to help you plan the teaching agenda.

Let's Dream Together

You'll need...
- Five sheets of newsprint, one for each group, titled as directed
- Pens, one for each person

It's always fun to think about possibilities. Many ministry teams take time each year to dream of what the ministry could look like in the future, though it's unusual to involve parents in the process. This exercise allows them to dream with you.

Divide the parents into five groups. Give each group a large newsprint sheet and a marker. Each sheet should be titled with one of these five topics:

- **Program** What could we be doing that we're not doing now?
- **Leadership** Who could do a great job ministering to our kids?
- **Facilities** What features could be changed to make an ideal place for our youth ministry program?
- **People** Who could we minister to in the future?
- **Flavor** What could it feel like for kids who come to our youth group?

Give the groups three minutes to brainstorm ideas on their topic. After three minutes, pass the topic to the next group. Let the groups brainstorm for three minutes on each topic as it comes around..

Collect the sheets for consideration at your next leadership team meeting (or Parent Advisory Council meeting, if you have one), where they will be processed and prioritized. Remind parents that dreams don't always become reality, but they do help us see beyond the immediate and into the realm of how things could be.

Commitment to Prayer and Encouragement

You'll need...
- **We're All Ears** (page 150-151), one for each group
- Stamped envelopes addressed to you, one for each family

Close the meeting by acknowledging the volunteers who sacrifice their time and energy for the ministry. If your volunteers are present, have them gather at the front of the room and ask a parent to pray for them.

Even if the ministry team isn't present, you can still end the evening with prayer.

Ask each of the parents to pick one volunteers to pray for and encourage during the remaining ministry season.

Consider using **We're All Ears** (page 150-151, in Chapter 9) for evaluation. You can distribute it for parents to fill out and return the following week.

Just before you dismiss parents, remind them of your willingness to talk about any concerns or questions and also of your support for them as they minister to their children.

Kids Today...

(see page 125)

Brainstorm endings for each sentence.

Kids today have a whole lot more...	Kids today have a whole lot less...

(see page 126)

Cut apart the strips. Arrange the items from top priority to lowest priority based on group consensus.

Participation in small groups for community and accountability

OPPORTUNITIES TO BE MENTORED BY SPIRITUALLY MATURE ADULTS

Activities teens will want to bring their friends to

Opportunities to develop student gifts and skills

OUTREACH TO KIDS WHO HAVE NO FAITH OF THEIR OWN

Biblical teaching, training, and discipleship

Meaningful service projects and missions trips

Wholesome social activities to keep kids busy and out of trouble

Here's What Our Kids Really Need!

(see page 126)

Circle five topics you think are most important for our youth group to cover. Rank those choices from one (most important) to five.

_____ Temptation

_____ Moral and sexual purity

_____ Family communication

_____ Basic Christian beliefs

_____ World religions and cults

_____ Occult and the spirit world

_____ Church history

_____ Spiritual disciplines

_____ Sharing our faith

_____ End times

_____ The life of Christ

_____ Money and finances

_____ Standing up for my beliefs

_____ Creation and evolution

_____ Peer counseling

_____ Prayer

_____ Defending our faith (apologetics)

_____ Biblical leadership

_____ How to be a good friend

_____ What the parables mean for me

_____ Denominational distinctives

_____ Dating

_____ Old Testament characters

_____ Honesty and integrity

_____ New Testament book studies

_____ Understanding the sacraments

_____ Culture and media

_____ How the Bible was established

_____ Grace

_____ Forgiveness

_____ Worship

_____ Preparing for marriage

_____ Other _____

_____ Other _____

Do you have other comments about the teaching we do?

Parents Advisory Council Member

Job Description

The Parents Advisory Council provides a two-way bridge of communication, encouragement, and support between parents and youth workers as we work together to help the students of our congregation grow into spiritually healthy adults.

PURPOSE

The Parents Advisory Council exists
- To promote effective communication between the youth ministry staff and the parents of teenagers in our church
- To provide support to the people and programs serving the youth of our community

QUALIFICATIONS

Members of the Parents Advisory Council should have at least one child actively involved in the youth ministry of our church. They should exhibit genuine concern for the overall youth ministry of the church and for the diverse community of students whom we serve. They should have a history of at least one year's involvement in our church.

TERM

Members will be invited to serve on the Parents Advisory Council for one year at a time with the term beginning and ending each spring.

EXPECTATIONS

- To pray consistently and specifically for the people and programs of our youth ministry department.
- To understand, own, and support the philosophical and theological foundations of the youth ministry of our church.
- To attend quarterly meetings as scheduled.
- To function as a sounding board for the youth pastor as vision develops.
- To accurately represent the voice of families to the staff and in the shaping of our youth ministry.
- To assist the youth ministry staff in evaluating existing programs and activities and in providing guidance as new programs and activities are envisioned.
- To develop an awareness of the concerns parents may have about programs, activities, and events of the youth ministry.
- To communicate the ideas, wisdom, concerns, and perspectives of parents to the youth ministry staff through the youth pastor.
- To communicate the vision, passion, strategies, and concerns of the youth ministry staff to parents whenever necessary, that is, to be an advocate for the staff and clarify misunderstandings should they exist.
- To assist, as members are able, with special ministry projects when additional adult involvement is advantageous.
- To manage the Parent-to-Parent Partnership mentoring program by identifying potential mentoring parents and connecting them with parents desiring mentors.

Dear Kwang and Julie,

Thank you for the consistent support and encouragement you've shown me as youth director since I arrived. I've enjoyed getting to know James, Andrea, and the rest of your family, since you've made your home such a welcoming place for the kids and me. Your commitment to your own family and to the young people of the church has been a real example to everyone.

Over these months of getting oriented, I've also appreciated your willingness to give me feedback and wise advice. Your understanding of the history of the youth ministry here has been helpful, as I've settled in. I think you've saved me from some blunders by sharing your perspective when I've asked.

I'm well aware that you are responsible before God for your children and that I'm privileged to support you in your role. It's important for me to have a means by which I can hear the collective voice of the parents whose children are part of the youth ministry program.

I would be honored to have you join a group (about eight to 10) of parent advisors for our youth ministry. You won't need to be involved in the week-to-week programming. What I need is your wisdom. The youth ministry team wants to listen carefully to the voices of parents. You are so well connected to other parents that I think you would represent their ideas, concerns, and expectations well. We also need someone to be our voice back to other parents. You understand where we're headed with our ministry, and we need people like you to be a voice on our behalf to them.

What I'm saying is that we need to listen and to be heard. You're parents who can do both.

I've enclosed a draft job description. I'll need the feedback of the group before we really solidify it, but it will give you the idea of what involvement with the Parent Advisory Council might look like.

Will you please pray about serving on the Parent Advisory Council? I'll call you next week to see what your initial thoughts are. Even if you can't get involved right now, I'd love to get your feedback on the job description.

The Parent Advisory Council will meet initially on March 22 at 7:00 p.m. at my home. After that we'll meet about every three months.

Thanks again for allowing me to serve your family.

Serving families for the kingdom,

Phillip Land

Youth Pastor

Chapter 8

Understanding Your Teenager 101

Educate Parents in Areas Where You Have Expertise

"Arrogance eliminates the joy of learning."

"Faith that has never experienced challenge has little chance to become vibrant."

(Pyramid diagram, levels listed bottom to top:)
1 ACKNOWLEDGE
2 AFFIRM
3 COMMUNICATE
4 ENCOURAGE
5 CONNECT
6 EQUIP
7 INVOLVE
8 EDUCATE
9 CO-NURTURE

Too many youth workers assume that parent ministry begins with sharing their vast wisdom, experience, and knowledge with parents who are desperately waiting for instruction. They think, "If only we could school these well-meaning, but obviously incompetent, people in the basic skills of parenting, maybe they'd finally end up having the kind of relationship with their kids that I would have if I were the parent."

Wrong!

If you've just opened this book and are starting to read here, may I respectfully request that you go back to the beginning to develop a sense of the prerequisites to parent education. Otherwise you may jump into attitudes and activities that can be more damaging than helpful.

Instruction in the absence of earned rapport is not often received warmly. It takes time to build relationships that can support the sense of intrusion that education represents, and it takes discernment on the part of the instructor to know what can be taught in any given relationship. For those of you who have worked through the process of building your parent ministry through the levels that have been outlined to this point, you're ready to build on the trust and respect that you've developed.

The critical issue in any parent education program is ensuring that the instruction comes from a competent, experienced, and trusted source. Even though you've become a trusted support person, you may not be seen as experienced in areas where you would like to give input.

Things Youth Workers Can Teach Parents

Assuming you've taken time to establish a relationship of mutual respect, you can begin to look for areas where your expertise can benefit parents. The instruction you present should be rooted in sound research, careful thought, and real-life experience. These are onerous-sounding prerequisites to be sure, but important topics a youth worker is qualified to cover.

You can't dump your load of wisdom on parents simply because you're able to put a checkmark beside each prerequisites on any given topic. One more issue to consider is attitude. Most of us have had teachers who were cocky, condescending, and patronizing. Their arrogance robbed us of the joy of learning. They might have had legitimate expertise, but without a sense of collaborating, the process is unsatisfying for the student.

Approach every opportunity to teach parents humbly. They too live with teenagers. In fact parents probably know a lot more about *their* teenagers than we'll ever discover. They have experienced a great deal in life. They have a deeply vested interest in the lives of their sons and daughters, so they're highly motivated learners. If we enter the classroom with a desire to learn together, we will benefit as much as the designated students.

Teach Parents about Adolescent Culture

Here's an area where youth workers are probably batting a thousand on the prerequisites for teaching. You've given the issue plenty of careful thought. You've studied the culture of your students—and probably lived it. This is a natural subject for youth workers to offer parents.

Because youth culture changes rapidly, presenting a fully developed curriculum for you to teach parents is pointless. You won't find much published on teaching parents about youth culture, because few authors wants to commit to a book that will be obsolete by the time it hits the bookstore shelves.

Don't despair. It simply means that you'll have the opportunity to develop up-to-date material, relevant to *your* community and uniquely yours.

Here are some thoughts on teaching parents about media and youth culture.

- The goal is to inform and equip parents, not to shock, demoralize, or offend them. There's plenty of material that will have them covering their ears and eyes at the same time. As you teach parents about youth culture make it your goal to present an honest picture without being overly dramatic.

TEACH THE TEACH

I highly recommend Parker Palmer's book *The Courage to Teach* (Jossey-Bass, 1997). Although Palmer wrote with vocational teachers in mind, even those who teach occasionally can learn a great deal from him.

- The outcome of educating parents should never be parents alienated from their kids. If our instruction results in parents becoming angry enough, they will simply go home to burn CDs and smash TVs. Give them a basis for meaningful dialogue with their children.

- Help parents realize that culture both shapes (directs) and mirrors (reflects) the values of a generation. Media *does* impact the way their children think and act. I'm constantly amazed that some parents see no relationship between the behavior and attitudes of their children and the music, movies, Web sites, games, magazines, and television their children are exposed to.

- Encourage parents to monitor their own media consumption. It's hypocritical to demand content standards for their children if they as parents watch and listen indiscriminately. I've seen plenty of parents who'll turn off the rock station with its music about sex and drugs and turn on the country station with its music about sex and alcohol.

- Help parents understand the power of the subtle messages in the media. Most kids are smart enough to filter out the blatant messages, but they are often oblivious to underlying messages.

Teach Parents about Adolescent Relationships

If you're a young youth worker, your own adolescent relationships are recent memories. You'll have a lot to offer parents as you share what you learned from your own teenage years. If you're older you've got years of observation and conversations with kids on your side.

Resources on Youth Culture

Understanding Today's Youth Culture by Walt Mueller (Tyndale,1999). Written for parents developing a response to the media their kids live with. Balanced, thoughtful, practical.

almenconi.com
Helping parents communicate values to their children.

antithesis.com
In-depth feature articles and reviews of modern Christianity, pop culture, and today's thinkers.

cpyu.org
(Center for Parent/Youth Understanding) Serves to bridge the cross-generational gap between parents and teenagers.

culturallyrelevant.com
Providing resources to bridge the gap between the culture and Christ.

family.org/pplace/pi
(Plugged In) Helping parents and youth leaders guide teens through the world of popular youth culture.

familystyle.com
Movie and video reviews.

gradingthemovies.com
Helping families find entertainment with values.

hollywoodjesus.com
Visual movie reviews with explorations into the deeper more profound meaning behind film, music, and pop culture.

pacificnews.org/yo
(YO!—Youth Outlook) *YO!* chronicles the world through the eyes and voice of young people—between the ages of 15 and 25—in the San Francisco Bay area. Integrating writers, journalists, and scholars with young people, especially teenagers in high-risk situations.

relevantmagazine.com
A look at God, life, and relevant culture from a Christian perspective.

screenit.com
Entertainment reviews for parents.

Relationships is one area that often becomes a battlefield for families with teenagers. Kids are going through the natural withdrawal process that comes with adolescence, which creates a great deal of confusion for parents who aren't sure what their new role looks like. Up to this point in their kids' lives, they've been able to guard them carefully from relationships that might be damaging, but now the stakes seem so much higher and the ability to control seems to be gone. Parents feel vulnerable and unprepared for the delicate balance of holding on while they let go.

In addition, the world of adolescent relationships is a foreign culture to many parents…different language, different rules, different customs. Like aliens, parents may feel unwelcome and uncomfortable entering their world. Family communication becomes dangerous, if not lost all together. When you help parents increase their understanding of adolescent relationships, you reduce the tension.

The following list of adolescent relationship subtopics make good individual teaching sessions or can be developed into a comprehensive workshop or seminar for parents.

- *The language of adolescent relationships. Each* generation has its own language for describing the unique dynamics and various levels of adolescent friendship. It's important for parents to understand this language —not necessarily so they can speak it, but so that they can listen in with understanding. Youth workers can often decode the language for parents who are learning a new relational vocabulary. This is especially true of opposite sex relationships where innocent-sounding designations often have deeper meanings.

- *Friendship clusters and tribes.* Adolescent relationships are far more complex than random groupings of kids who have a few things in common. When parents understand the value of tribal identity, the importance of music and fashion to identity, and the strength of adolescent friendship clusters, they're equipped to handle the intensity of the discussions that often surround the issue of adolescent relationships.

- *How friendships are formed and maintained.* What attracts adolescents to one another? What are the phases that friendships go through as they move forward? What indicates a friendship is disintegrating? How do adolescents respond to a failing friendship? When parents understand these dynamics, they can be more actively involved in encouraging healthy friendships and be available when times are difficult for them.

- *Current "coupling" rules.* Opposite sex relationships can represent some the greatest fears for parents, often because they wonder if they've done an adequate job of preparing their kids for that component of life. It's easy to shock and depress parents with gloomy statistics and anecdotes of disaster with this topic. Avoid the temptation and instead help them understand the dynamics and rules that exist in your community and ways they can guide their kids through these confusing years.

- *The value of knowing their kids' friends.* Enough said!

- *The importance of a welcoming home.* When parents offer a welcoming place for their kids to enjoy their friends, they become participants in their teens' lives rather than distant observers. Over all these years of working with students, one pattern emerges over and over: the homes where kids feel comfortable to be with their friends are the homes where parents and their kids are able to connect at meaningful levels.

    Offering kids a place to be with their friends is messy, expensive, loud, chaotic, and unpredictable, but it's one of the best gifts parents can give their teenage kids. Encourage parents to open their homes, their refrigerators, and their hearts to the friends of their kids, and everyone will relax just a bit.

- *The potential for positive peer pressure.* Parents need to understand the impact their teenagers can have in the lives of kids who are struggling. This represents a huge change from the way young children are parented, and it's scary! When children are small, parents protect them from certain relationships because they aren't equipped to handle the dangers. As kids get older, it's important for them to be released into potentially dangerous friendships so they have the opportunity to practice making choices before the consequences are severe. Teens *can* make positive impacts in their world.

Parents who have built moral values and spiritual strength into their teenagers' lives can find great joy in releasing those kids into a dark world to make a difference. Help parents understand that healthy kids will always have some friendships where they "reach down" to some who aren't doing as well as they are.

Resources on Adolescent Relationships

Web sites

The following sites, many sponsored by secular organizations, deal with a wide range of topics related to adolescent development and often lead to additional links.

aacap.org/publications/factsfam/develop.htm
Normal adolescent development provided by the American Academy of Child & Adolescent Psychiatry.

ama-assn.org/ama/pub/category/1979.html
American Medical Association's list of links to organizations that provide useful information and resources related to the health of adolescents.

canadianparents.com/teens

education.indiana.edu/cas/devtask.html
Developmental tasks of normal adolescence.

keepkidshealthy.com/adolescent/adolescentdevelopment.html

ncac-hsv.org/stages.html
Developmental stages of children.

personal.psu.edu/faculty/n/x/nxd10/adolesce.htm
Provides an introduction to adolescent change.

puberty101.com/

parentsoup.com/teens

Books

You can find many excellent textbooks on adolescent development. They're not cheap, but if you're serious about equipping parents with accurate and current information, they are a good investment. I'm particularly recommending two, along with several trade books.

Adolescence (8th ed.) by John Santrock (WCB/McGraw-Hill, 2000).

The Adolescent, Development, Relationships and Culture by Philip F. Rice and Kim Galye Dolgin (Allyn and Bacon, 2001).

Helping the Struggling Adolescent by Les Parrott (Zondervan, 2000).

Real Teens by George Barna (Regal Books, 2001).

The Second Family by Ron Taffel (St Martin's Press, 2001).

A Tribe Apart by Patricia Hersch (Fawcett, 1998).

Organizations

The Center for Adolescent Studies
School of Education
Indiana University
Bloomington, IN 47405-1006
Phone: (812) 856-8113
education.indiana.edu/cas/index.html
Advances the understanding of the psychological, biological, and social features of normal adolescence. The Center serves as a resource for information and engages in the generation of original research about the adolescent transition.

Center of Education for the Young Adolescent (CEYA)
University of Wisconsin, Platteville
134 Doudna Hall
1 University Plaza
Platteville, WI 53818-3099
(800) 208-7041
uwplatt.edu/~ceya
CEYA provides professional development programs and resources for those involved with young adolescents.

> **Rather than you telling them how they should parent, let parents work together in small groups to explore the implications of your teaching themselves.**

- *The spiritual value of expanded relationships.* Until teenagers experience relationships outside the framework of their faith, they have difficulty owning their own convictions. It's another area of fear for many parents. Parents incorrectly assume that their kids will always be drawn to the lowest common denominator when, in fact, faith that has never experienced challenges has little chance to become vibrant. Help parents understand the importance of allowing this exploration to happen gradually and within the safety of a healthy home, rather than guarding kids too tightly.

- *The risks of intrusion and the blessings of involvement.* It's always a matter of balance…that impossible blend of boundaries and freedom requiring daily adjustment and constant prayer. When parents understand how adolescent friendship works they are much better equipped to be involved in the lives of their kids and their friends so that the controls they impose are rooted in trust and mutual respect.

Teach Parents about Adolescent Development

For parents watching their little kids grow into little adults, the many changes make them feel like they're living with total strangers. The visible changes are often the easiest ones to cope with. The emotional roller coaster, the cognitive changes, and the spiritual transformations may represent the greatest challenges.

Parents feel like their teens are being transformed from beautiful butterflies into caterpillars instead of the other way around, but we know differently. We've watched lots of kids go through the adolescent metamorphosis. We've seen most kids come through the teen years as survivors with relatively little damage. We have hope. Not only have we observed the kids going through these years of astronomical change, but many of us have attended seminars and taken classes to help us understand the developmental realities of adolescence. We have a lot to offer parents about adolescent development.

Here are some areas you might consider covering in a series on adolescent development:

- *The dimensions of adolescent development.* Give parents a reminder that development occurs on many levels. The physical changes are obvious, but equally dramatic changes happen in other areas. Kids develop what psychologists call "formal operations," a huge shift. Emotional, social, and moral development must also be understood to appreciate the full scope of adolescent change.

- *Spiritual formation in adolescence.* The most important transition adolescents make is the journey from faith that belongs to parents to faith that they own, but in many cases little attention is given to guiding teens through this process. Remind Christian parents of the important role they play in the spiritual lives of their teenagers and to look for ways to participate meaningfully.

- *The interactions between developmental dimensions.* Parents need to be reminded of the complex interplay between the various dimensions of development: how physical development impacts social development; how social development impacts spiritual development; how moral development impacts social development, and so on. We tend to deconstruct kids to talk about each of the unique components of development without putting them back together.

- *Normal development.* From the day their kids are born, parents wonder if their kids are "normal." Pediatricians have charts and graphs for height and weight and age for walking and first words. The preoccupation with "normal" doesn't go away for parents of adolescents. It just becomes harder to define. We're able to help parents realize that normal is a much broader designation than they might have realized.

- *Gender-unique issues.* Gender distinctions become more pronounced during puberty. Parents benefit from training on the unique issues facing sons and daughters. Physical differences are obvious, but the relational, emotional, cognitive, and spiritual differences can be significant. This topic is especially helpful to single parents dealing with an opposite-sex child.

- *Talking to kids about sex.* Most parents have great intentions when it comes to talking to their children about sex; they just don't always do a good job. Organizations like Understanding Your Teenager and Focus on the Family, among others, offer excellent resources to help parents address this topic.

Adolescent Issues for Parents of Preschoolers

After about a dozen years of building relationships with the families of our church, I had heard one sentiment expressed over and over by countless parents of teenagers. "Why didn't anybody tell us this when our kids were little and we could have done something about it?"

Finally it hit me. I put together a two-hour seminar focusing on adolescent issues and invited parents with children under eight to come. I simply adapted material I had taught parents of teens on youth culture, adolescent relationships, and adolescent development and offered it to this eager crowd. My goal was simply to give young parents a framework for understanding issues they were beginning to face or would face in the near future. The response was overwhelming.

I also used the seminar to offer parents a basis to dialogue with spouses and with each other. An interesting side benefit of this exercise was that it connected (remember Level 5?) a group of parents who would increasingly need each other's support over the next few years of parenting together.

• • •

Together We Can Make a Difference

Become a True Partner with Parents in Their Ministry

9 CO-NURTURE

8 EDUCATE

7 INVOLVE

6 EQUIP

5 CONNECT

4 ENCOURAGE

3 COMMUNICATE

2 AFFIRM

1 ACKNOWLEDGE

"A servant attitude makes all the difference."

When I established the foundations for an effective parent ministry at the beginning of this book, I suggested that it should always be built on shared trust and mutual respect. When trust and respect reach maturity, the result is a shared commitment to the growth and development of adolescents in our care. It feels like a true partnership with parents. Jealousy and feeling threatened are replaced with freedom. The need to be needed is diminished, and the joy of seeing needs met is the new motivation. Instead of watching behind us for fear of being sabotaged, openness and satisfaction reign.

The benefits of partnership are certainly significant for parents and youth workers, but the real winners are the kids. They have the advantage of both parental and nonparental adult involvement in their lives without ever having to feel the pressure to choose one over the other.

This final level of the parent ministry process represents the natural outcome of working through the previous eight levels. The partnership that emerges is not forced or imposed. Parents feel they are appreciated and understood. Youth workers have taken the time to listen and have kept parents informed. A spirit of encouragement has marked interactions between youth workers and parents—who feel connected to other families with teens and equipped with the resources they need to do a better job. They have been given opportunities to be involved in the youth ministry in practical ways and have benefited from the expertise of others. How could that feel like anything other than a natural partnership?

Warning! It Ain't Instant

Obviously this sort of rapport between parents and youth workers doesn't happen overnight. (In fact, it takes more time than most short-term youth workers have to invest.) Be prepared to actively build trust for a few years (it may well take four or five) before you experience a consistent sense of mutual trust. But you reap plenty of benefits from each level of the process, so it's well worth the investment.

Warning! It Ain't 100 Percent

We may never click with some parents. For reasons we may never fully understand, they remain distant, aloof, and defensive no matter how hard we try to connect. It's easy to get discouraged when nothing we do makes a difference, but our responsibility is to affirm, honor, and encourage those parents even though they may never say thank-you.

Warning! It Ain't Easy

By definition a partnership always diffuses power. When we share responsibility, we lose some control over outcomes. It can be frustrating to make a huge investment in a family only to have it destroyed in a moment of parental thoughtlessness or anger. In our work with parents we may feel a strong urge to take back the program to manage it alone again. That's a good time to be reminded of Philippians 2:5-8.

It's that servant attitude that makes all the difference—but it's always the toughest part of ministry.

The Secrets of a Great Parent-Youth Worker Partnership

Shared Vision

When both parents and youth workers are focused on the growth and development of the kids they love, the partnership flourishes. Furthermore, parents who sense the youth worker is committed to their family's health the same way they are welcome the youth worker's involvement with their kids. And, of course, when a youth worker senses parents want the ministry to succeed, they have freedom to dream and even fail. A wise

> Your attitude should be the same as that of Christ Jesus: Who, being in very nature God, did not consider equality with God something to be grasped, but made himself nothing, taking the very nature of a servant, being made in human likeness. And being found in appearance as a man, he humbled himself and became obedient to death —even death on a cross!
>
> Philippians 2:5-8

youth worker will invite parents to participate in the shaping of the youth ministry vision and will regularly remind all parents of the vision.

Honest, Open Communication

Partnerships inevitably fail when communication breaks down. The importance of healthy communication between parents and youth workers cannot be overemphasized. The key to good communication is constant nurture. It's just plain hard work! When communication breaks down or becomes superficial and dishonest, relational disaster isn't far away. The Psalmist says, "How good and pleasant it is when brothers live together in unity" (Psalm 133:1). My paraphrase is, "How good and pleasant it is when parents and youth workers live together in harmony."

Regular Evaluation

When you're in a restaurant, the server stops by once in a while to ask, "How's everything?" or "Is everybody here doing alright?" Checking in with people before their problems become disasters is a mark of good service. We're servants. Get feedback through formal evaluations and informal interactions for a healthy partnership. Use or adapt **We're All Ears** (on page 150-151) as an annual parental evaluation of your ministry, but don't overlook informal opportunities to get feedback from parents. A teachable spirit goes a long way in building a strong partnership

Willingness to Forgive

When parents and youth workers make blunders and mistakes, trust needs to be restored. The easiest way to create a climate of forgiveness is to ask for it when it's needed. When youth workers model humility, parents find it easier to reciprocate. Don't be afraid to say, "I'm sorry." Chances are you'll need to be *forgiven* as often as you need to be *forgiving.*

Commitment to One Another's Success

Marriages work when spouses are committed to helping one another be their best. The same is true of the youth worker-parent partnership. My experience is that when we give ourselves to helping parents connect with their kids and helping kids appreciate their parents, parents will defend us, support us, and bless us.

Ideas for Co-Nurturers

Ministry mapping

On an annual basis—near the beginning of each school year—meet with parents to identify a ministry plan with desired outcomes for their teens. Ask these two questions:

• What do *we* want to see happening in your teen's life this year?

• How can we work together to accomplish it?

Parents who participate in ministry mapping appreciate the opportunity to have a voice in shaping the ministry strategies directed toward their child. Perhaps the goal for the year is in the area of spiritual disciplines. Parent can encourage their child and provide resources like devotional books or journals. Youth workers can teach on appropriate topics, hold kids accountable for their personal goals in the area, and establish small groups to help meet certain growth goals. A 15- or 20-minute meeting is adequate, so you can schedule back-to-back meetings over several evenings, easily covering a couple of dozen families. Parents and youth workers can encourage each other when they see signs of growth and development.

Common Ground: Issues That Affect All of Us

When we think about teaching intergenerationally in Sunday school or on a retreat, we gravitate toward topics that bridge the gap between the generations: communication or conflict resolution perhaps. These are worthwhile topics, but many others are equally relevant and can build relationships without addressing relational topics directly.

One of the great misunderstandings between the generations relates to the basic life issues each faces. Parents often see issues of adolescence as unique to that time in life, while kids can't imagine their parents dealing with any of struggles they face. Nothing could be further from the truth.

You won't find much ready-made curriculum specifically for intergenerational teaching, but excellent youth curriculum can be adapted to create an intergenerational learning environment that benefits both groups. Choose your topics carefully and shape your teaching to reflect your "hidden agenda": parents are still dealing with some issues they struggled with when they were younger, and teens are thoughtful about tough issues.

Structure your small groups in a way that puts several family units together for discussion and application. Help parents understand the value of letting their kids see them learning and applying biblical truth. Consider these topics:

- *Dealing with temptation.* Everyone faces temptations...for life.

- *Peer Pressure.* Peer pressure isn't just about smoking and drinking with school friends. Adults face pressure to wear the right clothes, drive the right car, and live in the right neighborhood. They want to compromise to have the approval of their friends, too.

- *Friendship and Loneliness.* Parents will do well to understand why friendship is so important to teens, and teens may be surprised to find that parents need friends. Maybe the reasons are more similar than anyone realizes.

- *Spiritual Disciplines.* A big issue at any age. What a bonus to have teens and parents encourage one other in an area that many kids assume their parents have down pat.

- *Worship.* Young people have plenty they can teach parents about passion and depth in worship. Shared worship benefits family relationships.

- *God's Will and Decision Making.* Kids sometimes assume their parents have already made all the decisions that need to be made, when discerning God's will and making wise decisions is a part of every believer's life, no matter what age.

What about moral purity, discernment related to pop culture, spiritual gifts, or evangelism? When parents and kids are learning together, they can hold each other accountable, encourage one other, and challenge one other. We simply need to give parents a little nudge in a direction they already want to go.

• • •

Not Without My Father

A parent meeting to corporately pray for our kids

Raising teenagers may be one of the single greatest challenges faced in a parent's "career." The need for unusual wisdom, patience, grace, and love quickly affirm the importance of calling for God's help. As a co-nurturer with parents, it's not only appropriate but also necessary for you to call parents to prayer.

It's important to establish a high level of trust between you and parents before attempting this session.

The *Big* Picture

This meeting provides a structured time for parents and the youth ministry team to join in praying for students and their families. The meeting is divided into four areas of prayer: worship, confession, thanksgiving, and requests.

Some Days

> You'll need...
> - Copies of **Not Without My Father** (page 152), one for each person
> - Pens, one for each person

Distribute **Not Without My Father** (on page 152) and say something like—

When I talk with parents I often hear them describing their feelings about being a mom or dad. On the top part of the handout, you'll see the categories Always, Often, Sometimes, and Rarely. I'm going to read a list of emotions. As I say each one, jot it down under the word that best describes your experience.

Pause briefly after reading each word:

worried	**hopeful**	**inadequate**	**competent**
overwhelmed	**relaxed**	**frustrated**	**wise**
alone	**involved**	**unappreciated**	**content**
disconnected			

145

Ask parents to draw a vertical line between the columns titled Often and Sometimes. Have them do a quick assessment of the words in each half and then share their observations. You can ask an open question like this—

> **What do you notice when you look at the lists you've created?**

You'll get a variety of responses, but you might hear some like these:

- I feel differently about each child.
- Sometimes I feel very positive and other times very negative.
- I feel like I'm on a roller-coaster ride.
- All the positive words are on one half, and all the negative words are on the other.

Affirm each response, acknowledging the variety of experiences and emotions people have in parenting. Read Isaiah 41:10.

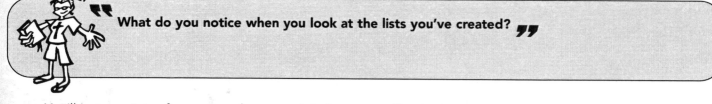

> **So do not fear for I am with you; do not be dismayed, for I am your God. I will strengthen you and help you; I will uphold you with my righteous right hand.**

Wrap up the opening activity by reminding parents that on this wild ride of parenting teens, God is anxious to ride with us and help us.

Worship: Acknowledging Our Dependence on Our Heavenly Father

> **You'll need...**
> - Bibles

It's appropriate to begin prayer with worship. Acknowledging who God is enables us to recognize his lordship and our dependence on him. This brief worship time helps parents focus on God as our heavenly Father.

Have parent volunteers read the following passages aloud (or project the text so everyone can follow along with the reader).

Psalm 103: 13-14   Our heavenly Father knows us intimately.
Hebrews 12:7-11   Our heavenly Father disciplines us lovingly.
Luke 11:9-13   Our heavenly Father provides for us generously.

Ask people to pray silently, thanking God for his intimate involvement, his love, and his generosity. Close the time in a spoken prayer or ask someone to close after a few minutes.

Confession: Acknowledging Our Weaknesses and Failures

A prerequisite for receiving God's help, humility is expressed when we acknowledge our own weakness. James talks about the importance of confession when we are requesting healing for sickness. The principle is simply that when God heals in response to our prayers, he wants people to recognize the results come direct-ly from him; people who have just confessed their sins to one another aren't likely to take credit for a miracle.

The principle applies to praying for our families. It's easy for us to assume that, when our kids are doing well, it's because of our competence as parents. Read James 5:16 to the group:

> **Therefore, confess your sins to each other and pray for each other so that you may be healed. The prayer of a righteous man is powerful and effective.**
> **Acknowledging our weakness opens the door for God to do something special for us. As Paul reminds us in 2 Corinthians 12:9: My grace is sufficient for you for my power is made perfect in weakness.**

Have parents break into groups of five to seven. Ask them to share about their weaknesses and failures as parents, in terms as general or specific as they are comfortable with. What they would do differently if they had the chance to raise their kids again? What patterns of relating to their kids that have been destructive? What regret have become clear to them?

After they've spent time sharing, ask one person in each group to pray a prayer of confession on behalf of all parents in the group. Explain that this way prayer is a reminder that all parents are equally in need of God's power to compensate for their weaknesses.

Be sensitive group interactions during this exercise, since confession can be a precursor to significant mutual ministry.

Thanksgiving: Acknowledging God's Good Gifts to Us and Our Children

You'll need...
- Copies of **Not without My Father** (page 152), using the opening activitiy
- Pens, one for each group
- CD of quiet worship music and CD player
- Transparency of **Psalm 103:1-3** (page 152), optional
- Overhead projector, optional
- Bibles, optional

Remind people that even when we don't pray, God is at work in the lives of their children because of his love for them and for us. Thanksgiving is an opportunity to share the good things God has already done for their kids.

Ask parents to turn to **Not without My Father** again to look at the second part containing categories of God's involve-ment with their families. Give them four or five minutes (with some background music playing) to think about each category and make notes about God's goodness in the area for each of their children. Parent may not be able to fill in each spot (although it might be surprising to see how many can).

Read James 1:17:

> **Every good and perfect gift is from above, coming down from the Father of the heavenly lights, who does not change like shifting shadows.** "

Have people move around the room to find one partner with whom to briefly share an item of thanksgiving from the list, and in turn, listen to one. Repeat the process with another partner, and so on until they've had opportunities for three or four brief conversations. Let people cluster in threes if you have an odd number of participants. The point is to verbally acknowledge God's goodness to one another.

Close this portion by having everyone sit down and read Psalm 103:1-13 out loud together. You may create a transparency from **Psalm 103:1-13** (on page 153) or read from Bibles if everyone has the same translation.

Requests: Acknowledging Specific Areas of Need in the Lives of Our Children

To begin, read Philippians 4:6-7:

> **Do not be anxious about anything, but in everything, by prayer and petition, with thanksgiving, present your requests to God. And the peace of God, which transcends all understanding, will guard your hearts and your minds in Christ Jesus.** "

Acknowledge that parents share many of the same concerns for their kids. Explain that you will mention a list of circumstances, one at a time. Parents who are in the circumstance can stand (or you may have all parents close their eyes and those in the circumstance raise their hands as an indication).

Then ask someone who has remained seated to pray for those who are standing. Add circumstances that might be significant in your setting or remove items that are inappropriate.

- Kids who are dating
- Kids who are spiritually apathetic or doubting
- Kids struggling at school academically or relationally
- Kids making important decisions about the future
- Kids who need physical healing
- Kids who are not making wise friendship choices
- Parents who are single
- Parents trying to restore relationships with a child
- Parents whose job pressures are taking time away from their kids

If you have time, have parents meet in groups of four or five to share requests and pray specifically for the teens of the parents in the group.

A Simple Prayer, A Hard Task

Finish the session by asking parents to write a short prayer on the back of their handout committing themselves anew to the task of parenting their children.

As you close the evening in prayer, include a moment for parents to silently offer up the prayer of commitment.

How are we doing?

We're committed to working closely with parents in their task of raising teens—YOU! Here's your chance to give us feedback. We value your insights and welcome your feedback.

Schedule and Calendar of Events
Can you keep up?

1 ├──┼──┼──┼──┼──┼──┼──┼──┼──┤ 10
too busy   about right   pick up the pace

Your thoughts:

Affordability
Looking for a bank loan to keep your kids involved?

1 ├──┼──┼──┼──┼──┼──┼──┼──┼──┤ 10
pretty steep   affordable   not a problem

Your thoughts:

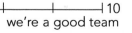

Relevance
Are your teens interested in the topics?

1 ├──┼──┼──┼──┼──┼──┼──┼──┼──┤ 10
not connecting   mostly helpful   right on target

Your thoughts:

Support and Cooperation
Does it feel like we're in this together?

1 ├──┼──┼──┼──┼──┼──┼──┼──┼──┤ 10
it feels pretty lonely   could use improvement   we're a good team

Your thoughts:

A Few Quick Questions

DO YOUR KIDS WANT TO ATTEND YOUTH GROUP EVENTS? TELL US
WHAT WE NEED TO HEAR.

_____ Do your kids want to bring their friends to
youth group? Tell us what we need to hear.

Does your family ever discuss topics _____
we're covering? Tell us what we need to hear.

_____ Do your kids have close friends in the
youth group? Tell us what we need to hear.

IS OUR YOUTH MINISTRY IN STEP WITH THE REST _____
OF THE CHURCH? TELL US WHAT WE NEED TO HEAR.

_____ Do you feel that your kids are safe in our
program? Tell us what we need to hear.

Are you kids being spiritually fed in our _____
youth group? Tell us what we need to hear.

_____ ANYTHING ELSE WE NEED TO HEAR?

Thanks for taking the time to give us your wisdom!
Let's keep working together to for the benefit of our kids.

By the way, you don't need a form to let us know what you're thinking. We like hearing from you!

Parenting teenagers is too big a job to do alone.

SOME DAYS

As you hear each emotion being read, write it in the column that describes your experience.

always	often	sometimes	Rarely

THANKS FOR EVERYTHING

	child's name	child's name	child's name
SAFETY AND PROTECTION			
PHYSICAL OR EMOTIONAL HEALING			
SPIRITUAL TRANSFORMATION			
PERSEVERANCE IN HARDSHIP			
IMPORTANT PEOPLE WHO HAVE HELPED			
UNUSUAL OPPORTUNITIES			
SPECIAL ABILITIES AND TALENTS			

NIV

Praise the Lord, O my soul;
all my inmost being, praise his holy name.
Praise the Lord, O my soul,
and forget not all his benefits—
who forgives all your sins
and heals all your diseases,
who redeems your life from the pit
and crowns you with love and compassion,
who satisfies your desires with good things
so that your youth is renewed like the eagle's.

The Lord works righteousness
and justice for all the oppressed.

He made known his ways to Moses,
his deeds to the people of Israel:
The Lord is compassionate and gracious,
slow to anger, abounding in love.
He will not always accuse,
nor will he harbor his anger forever;
he does not treat us as our sins deserve
or repay us according to our iniquities.
For as high as the heavens are above the earth,
so great is his love for those who fear him;
as far as the east is from the west,
so far has he removed our transgressions from us.
As a father has compassion on his children,
so the Lord has compassion on those who fear him.

Chapter 10

Outside the Lines

Parent Ministry in Special Circumstances

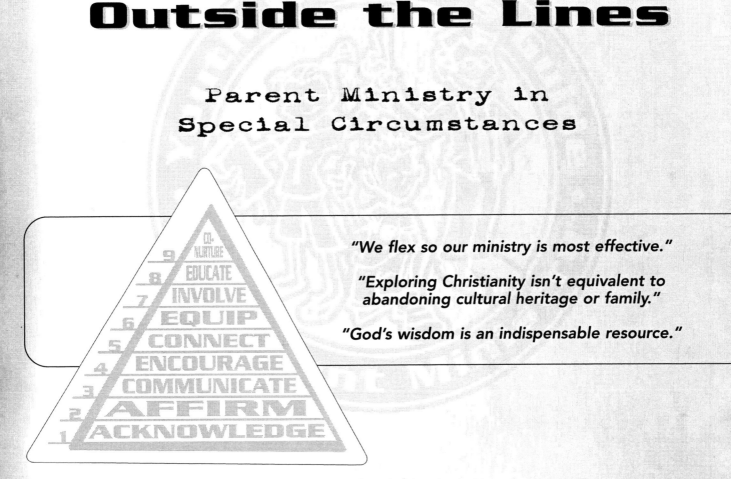

"We flex so our ministry is most effective."

"Exploring Christianity isn't equivalent to abandoning cultural heritage or family."

"God's wisdom is an indispensable resource."

- Jennifer is 14. She lives with her mom's ex-boyfriend. When he and her mom broke up six months ago, Jennifer's mom disappeared. Her bio-dad remarried 10 years ago, and her stepmom has never wanted her around. Her mom's ex-boyfriend is pretty messed up, and he's got a new girlfriend. Jennifer doesn't have anywhere else to go, so she's glad to have a roof over her head.

- Rahid is 17. His father, a leader at the local mosque, would be enraged to know that his son has been attending a small group in your ministry. He's told you that if his parents ever find out, he'll be disowned by his family. It could even cost him his life.

- Blake is 16. He's disconnected from his parents and wants nothing to do with them and their "stupid church." He's been attending Sunday school at your church and often stays for the worship service. You feel like he's beginning to soften spiritually. You'd love to tell his dad what's happening in his life. The problem is that his dad is the pastor of the "stupid church."

- Miguel is 15. His parents were killed in a plane crash two years ago. A few months ago he ended up moving in with his brother and sister-in-law who've only been married a year. They're finding it really tough to be "parents" of a teenager.

- Justine is 12. She lives with her mom. The good news is that they get along great. The bad news is that life has been tough financially—but they're working hard to make a go of it. Justine's mom works the graveyard shift, so it seems like she's always at work or sleeping. Her mom feels guilty about having so little time for her daughter.

- Courtney is 13. She just moved into the home of a great family from your church as a foster child. She couldn't stay at home anymore because her father had been sexually abusing her. Children's Aid took her away. She's an angry kid. Her foster parents are having a difficult time connecting with her. She only comes to the youth group because she has to come with the family.

Working with parents who live as husband and wife and lovingly raise their children together is a relatively straightforward process. The ideas and approaches in this book tend to work somewhat predictably in those circumstances.

But what about parents who don't fit neatly into the traditional box? You've just read a few examples of family systems that don't. Any number of special circumstances create challenges we must address. The remainder of this chapter identifies the most common scenarios we might encounter and offers some potential responses in each case as starting points.

Before we take a look, remember: the basic principles remain the same:

- Parents are ultimately responsible for their children.

- Our priority is to support parents in their role.

- Ministry is built on mutual trust and respect…and it will take time.

The parent ministry process outlined in the previous chapters provides a useful template for ministry in special circumstances, though in some cases we flex so our ministry is most effective.

Ministry with Single Parents

One of the most common family structures you will encounter, single parenting can be the result of a divorce, marital separation, or death. Some single parents never establish a permanent relationship with the child's other biological parent. Others

PARENT POINT

The burdens are twice as heavy and the joys only half as much fun when you have no partner to share them with.

Gerri, a widow with three kids

might adopt without being married. In spite of the noble efforts of single parents to make the best of their circumstances, most of these situations involve some level of disruption and relational trauma for the parent and the child.

Here's some food for thought as you work with single parents:

- Be careful that you don't make their singleness the primary point of their identity. Such narrowly defined labels create more restrictions than freedom.

- Don't establish support groups for single parents. They just feel more abnormal and ostracized. If single parents need support, facilitate mentoring relationships or integrate singles and couples into combined support groups.

- Integrate single parents with couples naturally and without awkwardness. Even acts as simple as how you set the table or establish discussion groups makes it easier for them to feel welcome. Avoid having groups comprising couples and one single.

- Be sensitive to pain associated with the circumstance that created their singleness. Death, separation, divorce, or abandonment all have an impact. The single parent may be struggling with issues of trust, shame, anger, bitterness, loneliness, grief, fear, or other difficult emotions. The emotions may surface—sometimes unexpectedly—in *your* relationship. Be kind. Be patient. Be forgiving.

- Recognize that most single parents (especially single moms) face difficult financial pressures. Do whatever you can to relieve the pressure through scholarships, fundraisers, and sponsorships. *Never* offer financial help in a patronizing way.

- Be cautious about sponsoring father/son- or mother/daughter-type events. You can accomplish the same thing with events called Guys Night Out, Flicks for Chicks, or other generic names that won't remind single parents once again of their "lack of qualifications."
  Encourage parents unobtrusively to take parentless children under their wings for the evening, inviting them along and then including them in the activities. Be extremely sensitive to kids who are parentless at intergenerational events. Do not single them out or say things that make them feel like leftovers or inconveniences: "Dylan, you don't have a dad, so you might as well just join in with Isaac and his dad. You guys don't mind an extra person do you?" *Ouch!*

- Make sure you're aware of custodial arrangements when parents are divorced or separated. You may be responsible for releasing minors only to legally allowed individuals, or you may need to be aware of which parent to call in a medical emergency.

- As you affirm single parents, be sure to acknowledge the extra work they do. Applaud them publicly—in front of their kids—every chance you get. They don't have another parent to make them look good to their kids; in many cases the other parents do all they can to tear down the ex. Again, be careful not to patronize or make singleness the issue. Just offer genuine affirmation to someone who can surely use it.

- Recognize your special ministry as an opposite gender adult in the life of the single parent family. As a male figure in the life of a fatherless girl or boy or a female figure in the life of a motherless young person, you have the opportunity to be a very significant voice in their development.

- Remember that single parents are often lonely and want to talk with you about their kids in ways that couples don't need to. Be patient as they vent their emotions or seek your input. They don't have spouses to share the journey with, so they seek someone genuinely interested in their teens.

- The most important part of the parent ministry pyramid for single parents is encouragement. You will never give them too much. Look for opportunities to encourage them whenever you can.

Enjoy the possibility of becoming a true co-nurturer with a single parent, perhaps the greatest joy in parent ministry.

Ministry with Blended Families

Blended families are formed when two family units come together to form a new redefined family unit. In most cases they involve a single parent marrying a new spouse, with or without a family of his or her own. The combinations can take many forms.

If one parent's new spouse has children, a new family of stepsiblings is established. If the other parent has remarried, the teen may have two families of stepsiblings to deal with. Living arrangements can be complex with a number of custody and visitation agreements in place. Extended family relationships may involve groups of people who have been previously unknown. New cousins, grandparents, uncles, and aunts. It can be confusing at times—especially to the youth worker trying to sort through the relationships. Working with parents in blended family situations has some challenges for youth workers.

Here are some thoughts to keep in mind when working with blended families:

- Many blended families manage well in spite of the hurdles they may face in working out the details of the relationships. Don't assume that all blended families are dysfunctional. Do, however, assume that children and parents in these reconfigured familial units face unique challenges.

- Don't assume last names within a single family group. Parents may change their names without changing their children's names.

- Don't assume that stepsiblings feel like brothers or sisters (or sons or daughters, for that matter). The dynamics of sibling relationships in stepfamilies are unique. Especially when families of teenagers are blended, teens often go through the rest of their adolescence without bonding to the other children or the new parent.

- Blended families face tremendous pressure to "make it work." Both parents and children may feel that they are betraying their family if they talk about problems.

- Don't pressure kids or parents to give you the details of, or the background to, their family's reconfiguration. As trust grows and relationships are strengthened, the story will emerge. Don't ask questions merely to satisfy your curiosity.

STEPFAMILIES

Dr. James Bray and John Kelly studied stepfamilies in the 1990s. "There are more than 20 million stepfamilies in America. For most of them the simple daily issues that challenge every family are even more anxiety provoking." The study goes on to conclude —

- A stepfamily has its own natural lifecycle, some components of which can throw the family into crisis.

- A stepfamily takes longer to develop into a family unit than was previously thought.

- A stepfamily is at greatest risk in the first two years.

- Some stepfamily forms are much more vulnerable to a second breakup than others.

- Successful stepfamilies accomplish four tasks:
  1. Integrating the stepfather into the lives of the children.
  2. Creating a successful second marriage and separating it from the first.
  3. Managing change.
  4. Developing rules for dealing with nonresidential parents and former spouses.

- A healthy stepfamily can reduce the scars of divorce.

From *Stepfamilies: Love, Marriage, and Parenting in the First Decade* by Dr. James Bray and John Kelly (Broadway, 1998)

- Stepparents often feel a huge need to be accepted in their new role. They often feel like failures in this capacity and need plenty of encouragement as they try to make the new arrangements work.

- As in the case of single parents, youth workers need to be aware of custodial arrangements and legal issues related to noncustodial parents.

- Most people have opinions on blended families—philosophically and specifically. Once a blended family is established, your opinion about its validity or appropriateness becomes irrelevant. You have an obligation to support and encourage the growth of this new family unit by applying all the components of a balanced parent ministry.

Ministry with Parents Who Are Unbelievers

If your ministry is committed to outreach (as it should be), you will soon find yourself touching families without a personal faith. Rather than assuming, like many youth workers do, that these parents are outside the lines of your ministry responsibility, I suggest they may represent your most fertile ministry soil. Many so-called church parents take the youth ministry opportunities their kids enjoy for granted. They *assume* you'll be available for their kids—that's what you've been hired to do! Although unbelieving or unchurched parents may be somewhat suspicious of your interest in their son or daughter, many can turn into avid supporters when they get a sense of your heart for their family and may come to faith as well.

Working with unchurched or unbelieving parents requires delicate balance and careful thought. The trust we build with them feels fragile at first, but it can pay big dividends ultimately. Here are some things to think about when working with unbelieving parents:

- They will be suspicious. As far as they're concerned, we're no different than the cults that have led many a young person off the edge of sanity. Allegations of sexual abuse by clergy casts distrust on us all. If we appear overly zealous or too eager to intrude upon their family, they may overreact. Patience is key. These folks have no reason to trust us—until we give them reasons over time.

- Some parents express their lack of trust by forbidding their child's attendance at church or youth group events. Do *not* advise minor children to disobey their parents. Encouraging teens to lie or sneak away sounds noble or spiritual to some, but it undermines the authority God has given parents and sends all the wrong messages to the teenager.

- If parents forbid their child from attending church events, find a way to mentor that young person in a less structured context. Encourage other students to provide spiritual support at school or in the community. Pray that, as the parents get to know you, they might allow participation.

- Do not create a us-versus-them mentality, making unchurched parents feel like outsiders. Sadly, the church has done a good job of making people feel sinful and guilty already. We don't want to reinforce the idea that they are "defective" people because they have not yet come to faith.

- No gospel message is more powerful than a changed life. When parents see positive changes in the life of their child, they are often more open to allowing the relationship.

- Treat unchurched parents like you would any other parent in your ministry. Affirm them to their children, and find ways to encourage them through appropriate notes and conversations. If possible connect them to other parents (Christian parents if possible) and communicate with them as you would any other parent. Invite them to your parent-focused events and involve them in ways that are appropriate. One dad in our ministry, who had absolutely nothing to do with the church, was thrilled to drive his van on many of our trips.

- Have several events on your calendar that are nonthreatening and appropriate to invite unchurched parents to. Don't give in to any urge to preach a sermon as soon as you have them captive. Remember, your ministry is all about building trust and showing respect.

- As their children come to faith, help those kids realize that their lives and attitudes—being the fragrance of Christ—will be the most powerful way for them to share the gospel with their families.

- The goal isn't to get unchurched parents saved; it's to show them Jesus.

Ministry with Parents of Other Faiths

One group of unbelieving parents that warrants special attention are those who hold to a different faith. With ethnic and cultural diversity increasing, this becomes a growing issue for youth ministries in North America.

In Toronto, where I served in a fairly typical suburban community, we had congregations of Muslims, Hindus, Sikhs, Jews, Buddhists, and Zoroastrians within just a few blocks. The schools our students attended and the neighborhoods they lived in reflected the same diversity. That meant we were routinely encountering parents who were staunchly committed to a faith very different from what their kids were hearing about at our youth group.

Ministry to parents in these circumstances can certainly be challenging, but here are some ideas to keep in mind:

- Understand the passion of these parents to raise their children with a shared faith. They are as committed to seeing their children embrace the faith of their families as any Christian parent is. For their children to become Christians represents failure as parents, so they may feel that you're out to destroy their family.

- Recognize the strong connection between religion and ethnicity. For many people, faith and culture are closely linked. Many parents are committed to preserving their ethnic identity, and the "intrusion" of Christianity represents a major threat to their agenda.

- Recognize the high view of family many ethnic groups have. Decision-making protocol, the role of father, and the place of extended family are just a few examples of areas to be sensitive to when connecting with families of other religions.

- Be careful not to belittle the faith of their families as you promote Christianity. They will quote—or mis-quote—you to their parents, and you may lose your chance for a relationship before you ever meet the family. They need to be drawn to Christ by the authenticity of the gospel alone.

- Be respectful of family holidays and traditions, which may be different from what you're used to. Exploring Christianity isn't equivalent to abandoning cultural heritage or family.

- Look for opportunities to meet the family when you're not wearing your pastoral hat—or clerical collar. Sports or community events provide a good neutral ground where your presence is not threatening—or is at least less threatening.

- Pray that you will have opportunities to influence without intruding. It's a fragile balance.

Ministry with Parents Who Attend a Different Church

Kids are often drawn to youth groups where their friends attend or where they think that their needs will be best met, so you're likely to have students involved whose parents attend a different church. This is more likely to create a problem with the leadership of the other church than with the parents, but it's worth think-ing through the issues as we consider parent ministry in special circumstances.

The parents in this category may well be Christians and desire for their children to grow in faith; they just aren't part of your congregation. What are some principles to consider as you think about your ministry responsibility to these parents?

- As a general rule, it's best to have parents and their preadult children attending the same church, where they can participate together in the life of the church and share a spiritual journey together. Don't lure students from other churches into your group for the sake of numerical growth. (Besides, it will create extra headaches if you're committed to family ministry.)

- Try to discover the reason for the teen's switch to your church. The reason may be innocent and need-based, but it may also point to other family issues that should be dealt with. As a neutral party, you may have the opportunity to facilitate healing in the family if that's needed.

- Be sensitive to denominational loyalties. Some parents are committed to their denomination and see their child's departure from their church as an act of denominational (and perhaps personal) disloyalty. Be careful not to belittle denominational distinctives or traditions. Encourage the young person to attend the parents' church on special occasions if this is an issue for parents.

- Get to know the parents by visiting their home or introducing yourself when you have an opportunity. Find out how they feel about their child attending your group. Answer their questions, and let them know of your commitment to their family and to them as parents. Let parents know you're an ally even though they don't attend your church.

- Treat parents who are comfortable with their child participating in your youth group the same way as you treat the rest of your parents: affirm and encourage them, invite them to your events, and establish a partnership with them in the spiritual nurture of their teenager.

- One final word on this: be sure to hold the students *from your church* with an open hand. If your ministry is not meeting their needs, it may be better for them to attend a different group in your community. Some kids are more comfortable in a smaller (or larger) group or perhaps a group more committed to a different aspect of ministry than yours, a place where their gifts could be better used. As you welcome kids from different churches into your group, be sure you also free kids from your group to go where their growth needs will be best met.

Ministry with Parents Whose Kids Are Spiritually Indifferent

Many churches have spiritually cold teenagers who are not involved in church life or family spiritual life. They are often antagonistic to the church and the faith of their parents. These kids represent a deep hurt for parents who have done their best to nurture faith in their children; they feel like failures. The pain is even greater for parents who realize they have legitimately blown it. They feel ashamed and alone in a church where the other kids seem to be doing great.

We may overlook these parents because we don't have relationships with their children. But these parents need our encouragement. As you think about ministry to this sometimes invisible group of parents, here are some things to remember:

- Feelings of failure and shame are sometimes converted into contempt and anger—often for your youth ministry. You might be blamed for the spiritual indifference of a teenager you've never even met. Somehow it's your fault because you haven't offered a program attractive to their child. There's no point in being defensive or shifting the blame back to the parents. Break the cycle of blame by focusing on the kid and looking with the parents for ways to connect.

- If there are any parents in the church who need your encouragement, it's these. Let them know you're praying for them and their teen. Tell them when you see any evidence of movement in their child's attitude or participation. Acknowledge the hurt and put your energy into bearing their burden with them. Let them know that you care about their child and share their concerns.

- Be careful not to give false hope or pat answers. Glibly quoted verses *(when he is old he'll return, or all things work together for good)* usually aren't helpful to people with this pain.

- Look for ways to be involved with the young person that doesn't involve participation in weekly meetings or special events. Stop in at the kid's work, get involved in coaching his team, or find a hobby you share. You encourage the parents of a wayward child when you get involved in the battle for their kid's soul.

- Let the parents know you're open to suggestions about ways you can help their teen get involved in youth ministry activities. Perhaps you can ask other youth group members to personally invite the student. Or schedule an event of interest to that particular kid—a skateboarding demo and testimony, a rock climbing expedition, or a sport's clinic. Parents may have ideas for natural connecting points.

- If the child's rebellion seems to be linked to obvious parenting blunders, the challenge of affirming those parents to their kid will be greater, but it's still important. Without trivializing the pain the teen may feel, do what you can to cast the parents in a positive light. Even the most deeply wounded teenagers, deep down inside, would like to have a good relationship with their parents. Build on that desire.

- In some cases the teen needs to awaken spiritually before family issues can heal. Work toward spiritual goals first and allow family healing to follow.

Ministry with Abusive, Unhealthy, or Highly Dysfunctional Parents

Some parents are clearly messed up. I can hardly believe some of the stories of abuse, control, addiction, and abandonment I've heard over the years…moms who are prostitutes, dads who sexually abuse their daughters, drug and alcohol addictions, physical and emotional abuse that makes my skin crawl. I could go on all day—and so could you. Our natural response doesn't always include compassion, care, supportiveness, and involvement. Often we simply want to rescue kids from the horror.

It's tough to work with parents who hurt the kids you care about. In spite of the contempt we may feel for dysfunctional parents, we may be in the best position to bring a measure of healing. Even in these difficult situations, we may be agents of restoration and grace.

Here are some things to remember as you wade into these complex and apparently impossible situations:

- Pray for wisdom. Did you hear me? Pray for wisdom. When you're dealing with the volatility of highly dysfunctional people, *you'll always be in over your head.* Each situation is unique, and you can potentially cause further damage. God's wisdom is an indispensable resource.

- Become familiar with local legal codes that relate to reporting abuse, age of majority, and so on. School counselors or staff members at the child protection agency in your region have the information you need. If you are the designated leader of your youth ministry, be sure all volunteers understand the law and your church's procedures.

- Establish relationships with important people in your local child protection office, police department youth bureau, school guidance office, crisis pregnancy centers, Alcoholics Anonymous and related support groups, and shelters. Keep a list of therapists and counselors (make note of specialty areas related to family intervention), family legal aid lawyers, and medical doctors. Copy **Community Contacts** (on page 165). Fill in the information and post it close to your phone. You have an advantage if you already know these people when you have a crisis on your hands.

Limit your long-term involvement with the counseling process, so you can remain a neutral resource for all parties.

- Don't ever assume a family is beyond repair. We may need to take radical steps to protect family members, but don't loose awareness of God's great love for all people and his ability to intervene. As much as possible, position yourself to be used by God in the healing process.

- Make an effort to get to know even the most dysfunctional parent. Often they have no one in their lives to give perspective or offer hope. Sharing common ground—their children—may open a door to help. I've visited parents in prisons, psychiatric wards, and their disastrous homes to try to connect. You never know when you might make a difference.

- Get both sides of the story in unhealthy homes. You will rarely find a family where one person is messed up and everyone else is perfectly fine. Listen to the whole story. Remain neutral if possible. I've found I'm able to be an agent of reconciliation by simply helping people hear one another's points of view.

- In dysfunctional family systems, one parent may also be victimized along with the children. For example, a physically abusive father is often an abusive husband. The victimized parent may need ministry as well.

- When you know a family is on the brink of a crisis, you may want to make an exception to your only-call-me-during-office-hours policy.

- If your community doesn't have a safe house for families in crisis, make arrangements within your church to establish several such homes. You may need a place for a parent or teenager for a few days while problems are being sorted out. You'll find making arrangements in a crisis easier if you've taken the time to establish possible homes in advance. Don't make the safe house locations public, or they won't be safe for the guests—or the hosts—any longer.

• • •

12-STEP PROGRAMS

You can find 12-step programs for many other problems beside alcoholism, some geared specifically to teens. You can search for links at www.geocities.com/stan1cel, by clicking on Program Websites.

Community Contacts

(see page 163)

ORGANIZATION	CONTACT PERSON	PHONE NUMBER	EMAIL ADDRESS
Alateen			
Alcoholics Anonymous			
Attorney or Legal Aid Agency			
Child Protection Services			
Christian Counseling Center			
Crisis Pregnancy Center			
Hospital Emergency Room			
Mental Health Office			
Physician			
Police Department (non-emergency)			
Police Department Youth Bureau			
School Guidance Office			
School Guidance Office			
School Guidance Office			
Suicide Intervention Hotline			
Teen Safe House			
Women's Safe House			
Youth Employment Agency			

The Effort is Worth the Trouble

Dear Ozzie,

This letter is long overdue, but we want to thank you for the difference you've made in our family. Now that Tyler has graduated, we won't be connecting with the youth ministry department like we have during the last 11 years. What a wild ride it's been! Thanks for being part of it with us.

When we moved here, we looked for a church with a strong ministry for our kids. The spiritual health of our children has always been our highest priority, and what we sensed when we came was that you shared our concern. Erin was just hitting junior high when we arrived. You and your team made her feel so welcome, it became the deciding factor in choosing this as our home church.

We felt so unsure of ourselves as parents when our children became adolescents. The elementary school years had been easy compared to what we were facing. All the changes left us feeling like we were messing up pretty consistently. Looking back on it now, we really didn't have a clue. We were glad we had you to help.

Thanks for your encouragement through all these years. Your notes and calls often came at just the time when we needed them the most. Thanks for praying us through those tough years with Kayla. Hooking us up with the Macfarlane's was the best thing you did for us. After what they had been through with Lauren, they had so much to offer us. (If our experiences can encourage other parents, you can introduce us. Payback time!) We're excited to have you performing Mike and Kayla's wedding!

Once again my friend, thank you. Thanks for the time you've invested in each of our kids. Thanks for the time you've invested in us! Your investment in families is paying huge dividends. Keep up the good work. We'll pray for you as you support and encourage another generation of kids and their families. If there's anything we can do to help, please let us know.

Bring on grandparenting!

Gratefully,

Rod and Alicia

"In survey after survey, parents emerge as the undisputed, unbeaten, and untied champions of spiritual impact on kids' lives. No one, no matter how megariffic their ministry, makes more of a difference than their parents" (Rick Lawrence, in "Looking Forward," *Group Magazine*, July/August 1995).

My prayer is that this book has helped you rethink the ministry of parents in the spiritual lives of their children and your ministry in the lives of parents for the sake of those children.

Now get out there and equip parents for ministry to their own sons and daughters!

Marv Penner
Caronport, Saskatchewan
Canada